DATE DUE			

Herman Wouk

Twayne's United States Authors Series

Frank Day, Editor

Clemson University

TUSAS 639

Photograph courtesy of Annapolis Capital

Herman Wouk

Laurence W. Mazzeno

Ursuline College

Twayne Publishers • New York
Maxwell Macmillan Canada • Toronto
Maxwell Macmillan International • New York Oxford Singapore Sydney

Herman Wouk

Laurence W. Mazzeno

Twayne Publishers   Maxwell Macmillan Canada, Inc.
Macmillan Publishing Company   1200 Eglinton Avenue East
866 Third Avenue   Suite 200
New York, New York 10022   Don Mills, Ontario M3C 3N1

Library of Congress Cataloging-in-Publication Data

Mazzeno, Laurence W.
    Herman Wouk / Laurence W. Mazzeno.
        p. cm.—(Twayne's United States authors series; TUSAS 639)
    Includes bibliographical references and index.
    ISBN 0-8057-3982-3
    1. Wouk, Herman, 1915– —Criticism and interpretation.
I. Title. II. Series.
PS3545.098Z77 1994
813'.54—dc20   93-29926
                                                                      CIP

10 9 8 7 6 5 4 3 2 1

Printed in the United States of America

For
Cindy, Paul, and David
and for the English Department Faculty
and the Brigade of Midshipmen at the United States Naval Academy

Contents

Preface

"Why would anyone want to write a book about Herman Wouk?" I suspect that question would occur to almost anyone involved in literary study. After all, Herman Wouk has been writing highly popular novels—that have netted him a fortune—for more than 40 years, and to date only one such book has been published. Compare that to the flood of scholarly attention given other contemporary writers—John Updike, William Styron, and Eudora Welty come to mind—or to figures of an earlier generation—Faulkner, Hemingway, Steinbeck—whose works were analyzed long before they had achieved immortality.

Further, one must wonder if Wouk's works are worthy of serious critical attention. The scholar who begins to collect criticism of the novels is sure to run across reviews by respected literary doyens, who have consistently castigated Wouk for a host of transgressions against literary good taste. Is it worthwhile to devote attention to an author who, in the early 1960s, provoked the following response, typical of highbrow criticism both before and afterwards: "Wouk is now a phenomenal merchandising success, sold as a detergent is sold. He can compete with the worst of television because he *is* the worst of television, without the commercials. . . : His readers really are . . . boobs . . . so 'starved for an interesting story' that they will ignore the reviews to read him. They are yahoos who hate culture and the mind. . . "[1] Can one imagine a more damning indictment of an author? The comments are reminiscent of that anonymous writer in the *Edinburgh Review*, whose scathing remarks were said to have sent John Keats to an early grave.

Nevertheless, there is no denying that Wouk *has* achieved a remarkable following among the American reading public. A significant number of readers have formed their opinions about literature and a host of significant issues in American culture and history, from works like *The Caine Mutiny, Marjorie Morningstar*, and *War and Remembrance*. Wouk's nine hefty novels—almost all of which would have comfortably filled three volumes had they appeared a century earlier—have been reprinted and sold by the millions, translated into dozens of languages, and on at least one occasion, served as examples of the best of contemporary American literature (in the 1970s, in the People's Republic of China).[2]

My aims in the present study are twofold. First, I wish to provide an assessment of Wouk's conservative ideology, tracing its roots and its flowering in his best novels. Clearly Wouk is an uneven writer, and to make too much of works like *Don't Stop the Carnival* or *Aurora Dawn* would be critically dishonest. On the other hand, Wouk's novels of World War II have attracted some favorable attention, and therefore they deserve some consideration as works of literary art.

I also wish to provide an overview of the entire corpus, and to consider the work of previous critics. I believe such a general survey has merit, since it has not been done before. One other book-length study, Arnold Beichman's *Herman Wouk: The Novelist as Social Historian*, was published by Transaction Books in 1984. This slim volume is valuable in many ways as a "source book" for biography, but as Jeanne Braham noted in her review, its "90 pages of text" stretch "uneasily between incomplete biographical snippets and plot summaries," with poor organization highlighting what Braham believes is a "superficial quality of analysis."[3]

Uncollected criticism of Wouk is scattered throughout magazines, newspapers, and literary reviews. No good bibliography exists to guide the reader through contemporary reactions to Wouk's novels. It is my hope that the review of criticism I have provided for each of the works I discuss will help fill this gap.

I have quoted at length from reviews of Wouk's novels, because I think it is important for an early comprehensive study to provide readers with an idea of the contemporary reactions generated by a writer's work. My aim is to give readers a sense of the breadth of such criticism, summarizing the strengths and weaknesses of each novel, as these were identified by Wouk's contemporaries. Consequently, I have not offered my own detailed assessments of individual novels (with the exception of *The Caine Mutiny*, *The Winds of War* and *War and Remembrance*). If Wouk is judged worthy of extended criticism in the future, other critics may find my efforts warranted.

In Wouk's case, the reactions of reviewers are particularly important, since the author has been sensitive to negative criticism. Though he has been known to say that he no longer reads reviews, the possibility of negative criticism still haunts him—at least indirectly, if my personal experience is any guide. I tried repeatedly to obtain permission to use the Wouk papers deposited in the Columbia University Library, and to obtain a personal interview with Wouk. Though I presented my credentials in writing, when his publicist learned that I was preparing a critical study, she denied both access and interview. The fact that I was at that time on the faculty of the United States Naval Academy, an institution that has traditionally revered Wouk and his fiction (where *The Caine Mutiny* has been required reading in many classes) made no difference; the door remained closed.

A survey of Wouk's works remains an important task because he is for the twentieth century what writers such as Dickens, Thackeray, and Bulwer-Lytton were to their own time: immensely popular figures whose writings influenced nineteenth-century readers and shaped the reading habits of middle-class generations. Anyone familiar with nineteenth-century reviews of Dickens's and Thackeray's fiction will recall that certain damning commentaries of their contemporaries suggested that these two writers would certainly be forgotten in the years to come. While I am not suggesting that Wouk will one day achieve the status of these nineteenth-century giants, I do not want to discount the possibility that his work may one day attract more attention and achieve more critical acclaim than it has heretofore received.

I would like to extend special thanks to the members of the English Department at the United States Naval Academy, whose support and encouragement sustained me during the time I was preparing this study and simultaneously running the department. Among many names, one in particular stands out: Michael P. Parker, whose cheerleading kept me going when the reviews became hard to find, or were poorly reproduced. I also wish to thank the members of the Nimitz Library staff, especially Katherine Dixon, for cheerful assistance in assembling the secondary source materials—no easy task, since no comprehensive bibliography of criticism about Wouk's writings exists. My special thanks go to Ann Kelly, my research assistant, whose enthusiasm and curiosity about the business of scholarship made the long trek from inception to indexing worthwhile. Finally, I wish to acknowledge the superb support provided by Warren French; one could not ask for a more competent and encouraging reader.

Chronology

1915 Herman Wouk born 27 May in the Bronx, New York, youngest of three children, to Abraham Isaac and Esther Levine Wouk.

1921–1930 Educated in public elementary schools in New York City; attends Townsend Harris Hall High School in Manhattan, for gifted youngsters.

1928 Rabbi Mendel Leib Levine, Wouk's maternal grandfather, arrives in New York from Minsk, Russia, and takes over Herman's training in Judaic studies.

1931–1934 Attends Columbia University, where he majors in philosophy and comparative literature; studies under noted philosopher Irwin Edman; graduated B.A. in 1934.

1934–1941 Works as gag writer for radio comedians; becomes staff writer for Fred Allen.

1941 Travels to Washington, D.C., to work as a script writer for U.S. Treasury Department's Defense Bond Campaign.

1941–1942 Joins U.S. Navy; completes Officer Candidate School at Columbia University; attends Communications School at the U.S. Naval Academy, Annapolis, Maryland.

1942 Abraham Isaac Wouk dies.

1943–1945 Serves aboard U.S.S. *Zane*, and later U.S.S. *Southard*, both destroyer minesweepers, in the South Pacific. Discharged from the Navy at the conclusion of World War II.

1945 Marries Betty Sarah Brown, a former navy personnel specialist, whom he had met in California in 1944.

1946 Son Abraham Isaac born.

1947 *Aurora Dawn*, a Book-of-the-Month Club selection.

1948 *The City Boy*, an alternative Book-of-the-Month Club selection; *Slattery's Hurricane*, screen treatment for Paramount Pictures.

1949   *The Traitor* opens on Broadway 4 April, starring Walter Hampden and Lee Tracy, and runs for 67 performances.

1950   Son Nathaniel born.

1951   *The Caine Mutiny*. Son Abraham accidentally drowns in Cuernavaca, Mexico.

1952   Awarded the Pulitzer Prize for *The Caine Mutiny*.

1954   *The Caine Mutiny Court-Martial* opens on Broadway 20 January, directed by Charles Laughton, featuring Henry Fonda, John Hodiak, and Lloyd Nolan, and runs for 415 performances.

1955   *Marjorie Morningstar*. Wouk visits Israel for the first time, as a member of a deputation from the American-Israel Society.

1956   *The "Lokomoke" Papers*.

1957   Wouk's grandfather, Rabbi Mendel Levine, dies in Israel.

1958   Wouk and family move to St. Thomas, Virgin Islands.

1959   *This Is My God*.

1960   Clark University awards Wouk honorary LL.D.

1962   *Youngblood Hawke*.

1964   Wouk and family move to Washington, D.C., so that he can conduct research for his novels about World War II.

1965   *Don't Stop the Carnival*.

1971   *The Winds of War*.

1973   Serves as Scholar-in-Residence at the Aspen Institute, Aspen, Colorado.

1978   *War and Remembrance*.

1979   American International College, Springfield, Mass., awards Wouk honorary D.Lit.

1980   Columbia University awards Wouk the Alexander Hamilton Medal, an award presented to a living alumnus for distinguished service or accomplishment.

1983   *The Winds of War* television mini-series appears on ABC-TV.

Chapter One

Life, Influences, and Ideology

The Writer

On 27 May 1915, Abraham Isaac and Esther Levine Wouk, residents of East 167th Street in the Bronx, New York, welcomed into the world their third child, Herman. The Wouks, immigrants from Minsk, Russia, would move four times during the next 15 years to various addresses in the Bronx, and the children—older brother Victor, sister Irene, and Herman—would grow in the bosom of this Orthodox Jewish family, learning the traditions of their faith and coming to understand the special status and burdens placed on them by their heritage. Abraham Wouk made his living in the laundry business, and in later years Herman remarked that one of his earliest memories was playing hide-and-seek among the laundry machines in his father's business. The future novelist would remember those early years as "depressing." He played the role of the "neighborhood fat boy, forever guzzling chocolate milkshakes."[1] Perhaps for that reason, or because of some unexplained attraction to the magic of words, Herman's literary interests began early. He was writing poetry by age eight or nine and had already developed an interest in drama.[2]

A good student throughout his grammar school and high school years, Wouk became a star in the minor galaxy of his own household, where his proud parents saw him master both academic subjects and the rudiments of his faith. The Wouks' kosher household afforded the youngster many opportunities to absorb the culture and heritage of Judaism, and to appreciate the particular history of the Jewish people in Western Civilization. Unlike many other Jewish writers of this century, Wouk has not lapsed permanently from the practices of Judaism. On the contrary, the demands of Orthodoxy still occupy the central place in his life. Thirty years later, he recalled with fondness his father's bidding $200 for the privilege of reading from the Book of Jonah at his synagogue's Yom Kippur service one year.[3] From an early age, he attended a Hebrew school after his regular classes. This solid background in religious training was further strengthened in 1928, when Mrs. Wouk's father, Rabbi Mendel Leib Levine of Minsk, immigrated to America and settled with the family in New York. Herman's Talmudic studies then began in earnest, and every day the young teenager pored over passages under his grandfather's watchful eye. As a result, his bar mitzvah, which he has described as a "major spectacle," afforded him the opportunity to give a "star performance" before his congregation. The grandfather was not fully satisfied, however, and lessons continued.[4]

Following his years in public elementary schools, Herman enrolled in the prestigious Townsend Harris High, a special school for exceptionally bright students. In 1931, his family moved from the Bronx to Manhattan, taking up residence on West End Avenue. Both the family fortunes, and Herman's, were definitely looking up.

After leaving Townsend, Wouk spent a semester at Yeshiva High School before entering Columbia College in 1930, Columbia University's highly selective arts and sciences college in New York City, where he majored in comparative literature and philosophy. As important as his studies were the friendships he made and the extracurricular activities in which he engaged. Attending college provided Wouk with many opportunities to display his creative talents: he wrote two varsity shows, edited the satiric monthly *The Jester*, and contributed a humorous column to the *Columbia Spectator*, the school's daily paper. At Columbia, Wouk's interest in literature and creative writing was encouraged by fellow student Arnold Auerbach, who later wrote two Broadway plays, *Call Me Mister* and *Inside USA*. Their association would lead to an important career choice for Wouk shortly after graduation.

Ideas were in the wind at Columbia, and like most college students away from the hegemony of strict yet loving parents for the first time, Wouk was attracted to new ideas. Exposed for the first time in his life to a large group of people who were not Orthodox Jews, he found himself giving attention to the ideas espoused by people whose intellects he respected. His close friend Arnold Beichman remarks in his study of the novelist that "Columbia was a powerful cultural influence which collided with Wouk's strongly religious background."[5] In *This Is My God* Wouk offers an account of his first confrontation with more "modern" Jewish notions. " 'The best thing we can do is intermarry and disappear,' a fraternity brother said to me. . . . It was the first time I had heard the slogan of assimilation spoken loud and clear. It froze me" (*TIMG*, 209). Assimilation, an idea prominent among many American Jews, who saw in it their best hope for advancement, meant abandoning the practices and traditions that set them apart from the mainstream. At first repelled, Wouk gradually came to accept many of the views of his more liberal Jewish classmates, and fell away from his Orthodox practices, not returning to them until 1940.

At Columbia, Wouk met the second important figure who was to have lasting influence on him. Irwin Edman, professor of philosophy, whose reputation as a teacher was legendary, took the young Herman under his wing. Through class lectures and many private meetings, he introduced Wouk to his particular brand of conservative humanism that was to stand beside Orthodox Judaism as a twin pillar of Wouk's philosophy. It was to Edman that Wouk turned for advice on both academic and personal matters, and he maintained contact with his mentor long after his days at Columbia were behind him.

When college was over, Wouk considered possible careers, and the family seems to have hoped he would return to school to pursue a law degree. It was not to be so, however. His good friend Arnold Auerbach, who had preceded him from Columbia into the working world, was employed as an apprentice for radio gag writer David Friedman.[6] Wouk's success with the Columbia varsity shows and his acknowledged ability as a comic writer (albeit an amateur) with the newspaper and literary magazine had convinced him that he wanted a career as a playwright. Since business for Friedman was good at the time, the gag man agreed to take Wouk on the payroll for $15 a week. The job proved to be far from glamorous: Wouk spent his time cleaning up dirty vaudeville jokes and recycling materials from old routines that Friedman hoped the public would have forgotten. After a stint with Friedman, Wouk and Auerbach landed positions on the staff of Fred Allen, one of the most popular radio comedians in America in the years before World War II. They started at salaries of $100 a week; before long both were making $400 weekly, high wages during the Great Depression. In addition to working for Allen, Wouk did some gag writing for Henry Morgan, another highly popular, iconoclastic radio comic.[7] By the end of his 13-year career as a gag writer, Wouk was commanding the princely salary of $500 a week.

Despite the long hours and the pressure of deadlines that both Friedman and Allen imposed on the two aspirants, they did not lose sight of their aim to break into Broadway. From March to September 1936, for two evenings each week, they would meet to pursue their dream, working on their own scripts and engaging in serious discussions about producing a Broadway drama (Hudson, 74). Wouk always knew that no amount of salary for his work as a joke writer would compensate him for the sense of anonymity he felt at being simply another horse in a stable of talented drays: the comedians who read the lines on the radio got all the recognition, and the whole ephemeral genre was intended to accommodate people's simple preconceptions and prejudices. Wouk wanted to be popular in his own right, and to achieve that popularity through more serious work that would bring his own voice as a writer before the American public.[8]

Unfortunately, the world was not progressing as happily as Herman Wouk during the turbulent decade of the 1930s. Like most Americans, Wouk watched with some interest as war broke out overseas in 1939. He sympathetically supported Roosevelt's policies that nudged the country closer toward entry into the conflict. In June 1941, he gave up his job in New York and moved to Washington, D.C., to work as a "dollar-a-year" man in the Treasury Department, where a campaign was being mounted to sell War Bonds. He even attempted to join the Navy before the U.S. entered World War II, but his lack of background in engineering made him an unlikely candidate for success in the highly technical environment aboard ship. When the Japanese bombed Pearl Harbor, the Navy did an about-face regarding applicants' proficiency in engineering. Wouk was admitted to the Navy's newly organized Officer Candidate School at Columbia University in 1942, graduating near the top of his class of 500. He was posted to the Communications School at Annapolis, Maryland, and in February 1943 received orders to report to USS *Zane*, a World War I four-stack destroyer that had been converted to a minesweeper. He joined the ship near Guadalcanal.

Aboard the *Zane*, Wouk served as the assistant communications officer, then communications officer, before becoming the ship's first lieutenant, a job similar to chief of supply and maintenance, which in the war years involved a great deal of scavenging and horse-trading in order to acquire vital ship parts and equipment, or various niceties to keep the men happy. Eventually he served as the *Zane*'s navigator as it traversed the Pacific, joining the fleet at such historic engagements at Kwajalein, the Marshall Islands, Eniwetok, and the Marianas. In 1945, Wouk received orders to join the USS *Southard*, another destroyer, as executive officer. He was later selected as commanding officer of this ship, but before he could assume command, the *Southard* was wrecked in a typhoon.

Service at sea during the war years brought Wouk a different kind of excitement than working in the pressure cooker environment of radio entertainment. On one occasion, he was almost blown off the deck of his ship; at the time he was certain he was going to drown, and he found himself thinking quite clearly that if he ended up underwater he would begin reciting the Shema, a short but highly significant Jewish prayer (*TIMG*, 89). Years later when Wouk looked for episodes to flesh out his "navy novels," he found his own wartime experiences fertile ground to till.[9]

Even in wartime, the excitement of combat and hazardous weather occupies only a small portion of a sailor's time at sea, and Wouk had opportunities to pursue his literary interests. He had brought along books that had caught his fancy, and restocked his personal library when he could. Aboard ship he read *Joseph Andrews, Nicholas Nickleby*, and— perhaps his favorite—*Don Quixote*, which he later described as "the key to my entire career" (Hudson, 107). ("I read it for the first time at 29," he noted, "and that was when I decided I should try to write novels.")[10]

Wouk also wrote regularly during his sea duty. In July 1943, he began a play about Madison Avenue radio advertising; three months later, perhaps inspired by his reading of Cervantes, he decided to convert the work into a novel; it would become his first published book, *Aurora Dawn* (Beichman, 21).

Late in 1944, while in port in California, Wouk met Betty Brown, a Phi Beta Kappa from the University of Southern California who was working as a WAVE. Though Betty was a Protestant, the two did not let religion stand in the way of love. On 1 December of the following year, Wouk was demobilized; nine days later he and Betty were married, she having agreed to convert to Judaism. At the ceremony she took the name Sarah Batya—"daughter of God" (Beichman, 15).

After his discharge, Wouk returned to writing for the radio industry, but he also pressed for publication of his novel. While still at sea, he had sent Professor Edman four chapters of his story about the advertising industry. Edman thought the work had promise, and when Wouk returned to New York, the Columbia scholar (whose nonfiction works enjoyed a considerable degree of popular success) arranged for Wouk to have lunch with Henry Simon of Simon & Schuster. Simon agreed to add the fledgling author's work to his list for 1947.[11]

Aurora Dawn began Wouk's success as a popular novelist. The American reading public was no doubt anxiously awaiting "new voices" to emerge in the aftermath of war; after all, previous conflicts had given rise to writers such as Hemingway, Fitzgerald, Dos Passos. Fortunately for Wouk, his book was picked as a Book-of-the-Month Club selection in

February 1947, assuring its arrival in thousands of homes and introducing readers across the country to this new voice in fiction. If not resoundingly positive, reviews were at least polite, and acceptance of Wouk's later efforts was virtually guaranteed. In 1947, comedian Fred Allen introduced Wouk to Harold Matson, who wanted to publish the young author's next work. Meanwhile, Wouk was working on plays as well as fiction, and in the decade following the end of the war, two of his works written specifically for the stage made it to Broadway: *The Traitor* in 1949, and *Nature's Way* in 1957. A second novel, *The City Boy*, was better received by critics but met with less commercial success. Then, in 1951, Wouk published the novel that was to assure his place in the canon of American popular writers: *The Caine Mutiny*. The book won the Pulitzer Prize for fiction that year. A play by Wouk, based on the novel, became a long-running Broadway production; the movie version, starring Humphrey Bogart, won Academy awards. Captain Queeg joined Huckleberry Finn and Captain Ahab in the pantheon of memorable figures in American fiction.

In the 1950s, the Wouks moved to Fire Island, New York, where Wouk continued his career as a novelist. The family began growing, too, but tragedy struck while the Wouks were on vacation in Mexico. In what Wouk described as a "tragic and senseless" accident, their eldest son Abraham drowned in a swimming pool shortly before his fifth birthday.[12]

Meanwhile, Wouk was becoming a public figure. In June 1953, he delivered the commencement address at Yeshiva College in New York, where for several years during the 1950s he taught a fall-semester course in English composition. He considered his students "the most hard-driven in the world," largely because they were trying to manage the double task of studying for the ministry while obtaining a college education—both full-time pursuits (*TIMG*, 184). In 1955, Wouk went as part of an American delegation to Israel, then celebrating the seventh anniversary of its independence. While there, he and his wife visited David Ben-Gurion at his retreat in the Negev desert. The impressions of this trip were significant: they may well have spurred him to write his only work of nonfiction, *This Is My God* (1959), an explanation of Orthodox Judaism for nonbelievers; and they provided material for passages of *Inside, Outside* (1985), a novel written some three decades later.[13]

Two major novels appeared in the next 10 years: *Marjorie Morningstar* (1955) and *Youngblood Hawke* (1962). Both were best-sellers, assuring Wouk an income that allowed him to pursue his career unimpeded and in the fashion he preferred. His regular work habits—he wrote every morning, in longhand on yellow pads, and spent some part of almost every day writing copious notes to himself—included time to celebrate his religion in the fashion his grandfather had taught him.[14] In 1958 the family moved to St. Thomas in the U.S. Virgin Islands. The experience provided Wouk with material for yet another novel, *Don't Stop the Carnival* (1965), perhaps the least successful of Wouk's books.

He had hardly finished it when he turned his attention once again to World War II, this time planning a multi-volume novel that would focus on the sacrifices of those who went to war to protect democracy and to recount the horrors visited upon the Jews by Hitler and the Nazis. So that he could guarantee historic authenticity for this work, in 1964 Wouk moved to Washington, D.C., where he obtained a townhouse in the fashionable Georgetown district. The work he had set out for himself would occupy the next 14 years. From 1965 until well into the 1970s, he spent much time doing research in the National Archives and other repositories in Washington and elsewhere, and interviewing people who had firsthand knowledge of World War II, or who were experts on German culture (Beichman, 81–82). The efforts produced two works each totalling over 1,000 pages: *The Winds of War* (1971) and *War and Remembrance* (1978). Even after publication, these stories continued to be a part of his life, as he supervised production of scripts for two television mini-series based on these historical romances.

Unlike most popular American writers, Wouk did not capitalize on the commercial possibilities available to him as a result of his success. He avoided most public appearances and was noticeably absent from late-night radio and television talk shows, where many novelists plug their latest releases and offer insights into their private selves. This is not to say that Wouk remained a recluse. He and his wife attended a state dinner at the Johnson White House in 1965 (Beichman, 14), and in 1973 he spent the summer as a scholar-in-residence at the Aspen Institute in Colorado. In the fall of 1981, the Wouks were again guests of the president at a White House function honoring Israeli Prime Minister Menachim Begin. In November of the following year, the Wouks visited the People's Republic of China as guests of the Chinese Writers Association. At that time, he was the most widely published American writer in China (Beichman, 77). Wouk spent his time in the early 1980s shuttling between Georgetown and California, working on the television productions of *The Winds of War*, released in 1983 to exceptional popular acclaim and respectably high Neilson ratings, and then *War and Remembrance*, a 1988–89 release that generated less public response.

Wouk's Ideology

As T. S. Eliot has reminded us, no writer produces his work without
some acknowledgment of literary tradition. It has long been customary
to look to an artist's biography for the people and works that influenced
the production of his or her art. Literary tradition has a strong hand in
shaping Herman Wouk's novels. He has consciously worked within a
specific tradition, while rejecting another. At the same time, two powerful figures have had significant impact in shaping his ideology: his
grandfather, Rabbi Mendel Levine, and his Columbia philosophy professor, Irwin Edman. While specific literary influences will be discussed in
relation to each of Wouk's novels, here it seems pertinent to examine his
ideas about the novel in more general terms, and to outline the forma-
tion of his political and moral conservatism.

By his own admission, Wouk has worked under the powerful influence of writers as diverse as Leo Tolstoy, Mark Twain, Ring Lardner,
Robert Benchley (author of *Life with Father*), and E. B. White. He has
been especially influenced by Miguel de Cervantes, Charles Dickens, and
Anthony Trollope (Hudson, 60–61). The list is revealing. Many of these
writers possess a comic vision of life. Many wrote long, rambling, multi-
layered narratives that attempt to portray an entire society. Most were
particularly sensitive to the demands of a large reading public, which
included refraining from both the use of "objectionable" language and
the representation of taboo scenes (such as specific descriptions of sexual
encounters).[15] These qualities appealed to Wouk early in his career, as he
attempted to capture an audience for his writings. He admired Twain, he
once said, because he had the ability to "express everything we have to
say in the framework of a very limited vocabulary in the interests of honesty and authenticity."[16] Early in his career, Wouk was so intent on
avoiding language and incident which might cause offense that he even
included an explanatory note in *The Caine Mutiny*, outlining his reasons
for avoiding the graphic language often spoken by sailors.[17]

If certain writers had a positive impact on Wouk, others left an equally strong negative impression. Modernist authors did not appeal to him.
He found in writers such as Marcel Proust and James Joyce only confusion and diminution of what he considered to be the writer's true task.
With their insistence on technique and style and their exploration of the
psychological dimension of character, these writers were removing the
novel from the hands of the common reader and making it the preserve
of cognoscenti. In his notebooks, public pronouncements, and fiction, he

repeatedly notes the "damage" done to the novel by the modernist movement. For Wouk, the achievement of the form lay in creating a world of characters whose actions and statements were explicitly linked to their inner motivations, and in creating a seamless facade of reality. Hence, Wouk consciously set himself apart from a great many contemporaries, by modeling his work on that of the great eighteenth- and nineteenth-century novelists. To read *The City Boy* is to reenter the novel as Mark Twain imagined it; to move through the intricate plots of *The Caine Mutiny*, or *Marjorie Morningstar*, or *Youngblood Hawke*, gives aficionados of the fiction of Dickens or Trollope a sense of déjà vu; experiencing World War II through the eyes of the Henry family in *The Winds of War* and *War and Remembrance* evokes not Proust's *Remembrance of Things Past*, but Tolstoy's *War and Peace*—or, for many American readers, Margaret Mitchell's *Gone with the Wind*.

It is not surprising that Wouk should choose traditional models for his fiction, for his vision of society is essentially conservative. Wouk himself once observed that "my career has been a sort of vector" between "two forces—Edman and Granpa."[18] To these two powerful influences I would add a third: his naval service during World War II. To fully understand both Wouk's achievement as a novelist, and what some critics have categorized as his major faults, it is necessary to appreciate the lessons he learned from these two men, and to gain a sense of how the war affected his attitudes about his country and himself.

The most powerful figure in the Wouk family was clearly Mendel Leib Levine. Born and raised in Minsk, Russia, Levine studied at the famous Volozin Yeshiva in Lithuania, and became one of the most important rabbis in his native city. Even after the Bolsheviks came to power, he remained in his homeland, finally emigrating to America to join his daughter and her family only in 1928, when conditions for intellectuals began rapidly deteriorating in Russia. His first task—a self-appointed one, apparently—was to turn his youngest grandchild into a Talmudic scholar. Wouk once recalled that, almost immediately upon his grandfather's arrival in their household, he had taken the 13-year-old youngster aside and said to him in emphatic Russian, "*Za rabotu!*" ("To work!"). Wouk spent many long hours poring over pages of the Talmud, working through abstruse conundrums posed by Jewish thinkers for over a millennium. Grandfather Levine was a hard taskmaster, and the Talmud no easy code to crack; sometimes Herman spent a month on a single page (*TIMG*, 157). To make matters even more difficult, Grandfather Levine spoke no English when he arrived in America, only a bit of Russian, and a Russian version of Yiddish. How they managed to communicate "remains a mystery to me," Wouk notes in his reminiscence of his grandfather; but he admits "in my whole lifetime nobody has communicated to me more effectively . . . " (*TIMG*, 158).

Rabbi Levine communicated to his grandson a deep love for his religion and his sense of identity as a Jew. That emotional attachment was supplemented with a firm intellectual grounding in the traditions and practices of the faith, so that Herman not only felt strongly about his religion, but he understood the reasons for many of the ceremonies and requirements that seemed so strange to outsiders. No doubt thoughts of this grandfather and the lessons learned at his side were responsible for Wouk's return to his faith in 1940, after a brief lapse following his years at Columbia.[19]

Orthodoxy—especially Jewish Orthodoxy—implies rules. Those who practice it commit themselves to conformity—anathema to the modernist position that fulfillment in life is found through the attainment of individuality. Wouk takes great pride in being one who fits within the system he has adopted. For him, there is no stigma attached to being a cog in a wheel, a member of a team, a participant in a community exercise. He does not praise the Romantic desire to strike out on one's own, to reject society in favor of self-fulfillment. On the contrary, his fiction is a litany of praise for those who can subordinate self-interest to larger causes. Clearly, a great deal of that attitude comes from the ideals of Orthodoxy.[20]

Just as important, however, in shaping Wouk's outlook on the proper role of man in society was his contact with Irwin Edman. A man Wouk described as "a naturalistic skeptic of the deepest die," Edman's brand of conservative individualism meshed curiously with Wouk's sense of the necessity for subordination of self to larger goals.[21] It is wrong to assume that Wouk turned his back on intellectualism to find a popular brand of conservatism. Many of his ideas come from Edman, a respected academic with a popular following achieved largely through the publication of several collections of essays for the general reader, most notably *Philosopher's Holiday* (1938).[22] It is not surprising that Wouk should have been drawn to Edman. As Charles Frankel observes in his introduction to a collection of Edman's work: "Probably no teacher in the 200-year history of Columbia drew more affection to himself from his students; and no professor of philosophy in recent years has succeeded quite so well in domesticating the idea of philosophy on the American scene."[23] Edman was a remarkably effective teacher, who taught "as much by the contagion of his personality . . . as by the lucidity and sympathy he brought to the statement of a philosophical position" (Frankel, 1). In outlook, he was "radically orthodox," speaking out for "the old, central truths to which human beings have been recurrently led when they have looked beyond the fashions and have been honest, humble, and clear-headed" (Frankel, 8–9). Certainly this is the position Wouk takes in vir-tually all of his writings: he trusts his readers to see beyond faddishness to the essential qualities that distinguish humans from brutes.

From Edman, too, Wouk learned to prize the arts—literature, paint-ing, sculpture—as important in both life and philosophy. Edman's brand of art appreciation was based on moral as much as aesthetic principles: art was to serve higher aims, not simply be beautiful. In "Art for Philistia," the Columbia philosopher lashes out at those "prophets of sen-sitive despair" who, following the lead of modernists such as Walter Pater, abandon traditional art and values: they have decided that "what is good is not what is commanded by a law no longer believed in. What is good is what is moving to the senses, emotions, and the mind" (Edman 1929, 133). Edman considers this attitude totally fallacious, as he explains in another essay: "it is the fallacy of the usual sensualist and the routine aesthete . . . to think of sensations, barbarous or refined, as detachable and atomic things" (Edman 1931, 185). For him, there is much more to life than mere animate sensation, as he explains with a rather amusing analogy: "To describe or to face experience in terms only of its physical and animal machinery is no more complete or relevant than it would be to describe a charming dinner party by talking exclu-sively about the digestive processes of the guests" (Edman 1929, 168).

One can detect a similar stance in virtually all of Wouk's major nov-els, where the antiheroes—Tom Keefer in *The Caine Mutiny*, Noel Airman in *Marjorie Morningstar*, Mrs. Winters in *Youngblood Hawke*—place their hopes for personal fulfillment in attainment of sensual satia-tion, only to be frustrated in the effort to achieve any personal peace or satisfaction. These characters have parallels in the works of Wouk's con-temporaries, many of whose attitudes and methods he found wanting.[24] This tendency to castigate the modern was certainly fostered by Edman, who offers this stinging critique of the modernist spirit and its heroes in a 1924 defense of traditional values:

> . . . having discarded the old myths, we have gradually been forming a hero-myth of our own. He—or she—we thank the stars . . . is no hero . . . It makes no difference whether [the modern "hero"] be a man or

woman. In either case, the ideas, like the figure and headdress, will be much the same. He will not talk of love or admit it. He will not believe in the Good Life or be publicly seen leading it. . . . He will try to be a tough mind gayly indifferent in a tough world. The last obscenity he will permit himself will be nobility. The last weakness he will indulge in will be to be sweet or soft. He will talk like a character out of Ernest Hemingway, act like one of Aldous Huxley's bizarre London intelligentsia . . . and try to think in such terms as James Joyce's heroines use in their more untrammeled moments. (Edman 1929, 204–05)

Edman believed that the "art of literature" in the modernist age had degenerated into "a study of clay feet," while poetry had become "a thin playing with irrelevant verbal music" (Edman 1929, 135)—sure signs of growing antiheroism and an unwillingness to confront important social issues. Citing Hemingway's heroes as examples, Edman criticizes modernist writers who indulge in "a new kind of naïveté," that consists in "avoiding articulateness," "dodging sentiment" and "avoiding thought." Those who seek solace in such art are engaging in a flight "from the complexities of existence"; the "important and the safe thing" for devotees of modernism "is to be interested but not possessed" (Edman 1931, 153).

Who is it that seeks the pleasures of such dilettantism? Certainly not the common man: "the average man in the street has become increasingly suspicious of and insensitive to art as a thing, a life, a cult." In the view of mainstream America, art "is a foolish epithet adored by effeminate sillies . . . profound, unctuous, and essentially unimportant."[25] Edman does have some good words for Proust and Joyce, citing their power to evoke response and provide insight into the human condition, but such praise pales by comparison with his denunciation of the flight from responsibility that he finds in most artists of the first half of the twentieth century. The pages of Wouk's fiction, and the transcripts of interviews with him, reflect the influence of Edman's ideas about both the philosophical evils of modernism and the catastrophe for art that the abandonment of traditional forms entails.

Several of Edman's ideas affected Wouk with similar force, most importantly, a distaste for and distrust of Freudian psychology. Edman associated the evils of "popular intellectualism" with what he called a "central faith" in "the efficacy of 'psychology' " (Edman 1929, 92). He classified among the "enemies of the soul of man" the "new psychologies," "especially as practiced . . . by men of letters," because they make man lose respect for his spiritual side and cause him to become "incredibly scornful of his own idealism." Instead of showing man how he is different from other creatures, the practitioners of this black art "teach us to range ourselves with apes and peacocks rather than with heroes and angels" (Edman 1931, 8–9).

This reactionary view—reminiscent of many of the critiques of Darwinian science half-a-century before—becomes almost vitriolic in some of Edman's prose. "Lo, the libido! Hail the unconscious!" he carps in an early essay, mocking this "grand new insight" that has "cleansed" the "rottenness" from the human spirit. This "fad"—which Edman distinguished from real psychology—that reduced every human impulse to the sex drive, "is not science at all, but magic of a peculiarly pernicious sort" (Frankel, 92). Edman is genuinely concerned about the reductive nature of Freudianism. "It must be remembered," he cautions his readers in *The Contemporary and His Soul*, "that in the old mystery religions no orgy really saved anybody"; the free practice of sexual activity offers at best temporary release from life's woes, and turns out to be "simply another hectic avenue to disillusion" (Frankel, 149).

In place of modernist tendencies to glorify sensation and psychology as explanations for the human condition, Edman urges a return to the study of traditional values. Conservative in his stance, he opts for what he sees his contemporaries as vilifying: values such as patriotism, loyalty, devotion to family, love of neighbor and of country (Edman 1929, 193). The movement toward "idol smashing" is nothing new; he notes its persistence in society since the medieval period, but argues that in the first quarter of the twentieth century "that exciting enterprise has become incredibly exaggerated" (Edman 1929, 159). For him, the problem that every intelligent person of this century faces involves accommodating the new sophistication that has come from advances in knowledge (especially scientific knowledge), with eternal verities of the human condition. "The question indeed comes down to this: Is it possible to be at once sweet and sophisticated? In our generation can one be at once honest and kindly, intelligent and courteous, informed and gay? Is the price of modern knowledge ill humor and ill temper? Must we pay for having eaten of the tree of good and evil by losing our heritage of urbanity and our saving faith in people and things? Is this the folly that one calls being wise?" (Edman 1929, 208). Edman—and Wouk was to follow him in this—placed his faith in the common man to overcome a blind commitment to scientific truths. "The prestige of science has misled us," he concludes, into believing that there is "something more metaphysically respectable about atoms than about ambitions"; but "the common man knows better and the scientists are beginning to." The discoveries about the physical world are "the formulas, not the stuff, of our experience" (Edman 1929, 199–200).

Many of the strong feelings about marriage and family that permeate Wouk's works reflect the strident pronouncements on these subjects that appear throughout Edman's writings. "For the majority of men and women," Edman remarks in *The Contemporary and His Soul*, "the need for an intimate sharing of life" is "best found in the institution of marriage"; the "good citizen" and "good father" have "sources of vital restoration" at which intellectuals can only scoff in vain (Edman 1929, 181).

For Wouk, Edman's most important philosophical tenet was perhaps his belief in the limits of personal liberty and individual freedoms. Already predisposed to accept conformity by the Orthodox training that he received from his grandfather, Wouk would no doubt have responded sympathetically to statements such as these:

> To have a fixed, though humble place in an established order, to be able to act calmly with reference to one code assumed . . . to be reasonable and good, these are the rewards of acceptance. (Edman 1931, 35) . . . it requires not the preaching of a moralist but the unmistakable nature of things to show us that absolute liberty is impossible. We may resent the false, outworn, and unnecessary repressions that parents and teachers have forced upon us. But some order or organization of life is indispensable if we are to live at all or live at all happily. (Edman 1929, 170)

Belief in traditional values; submission to just authority; acceptance of restraints on personal freedoms for some greater good. These are the tenets of a faith that Herman Wouk learned at the side of his grandfather the rabbi, and from the lips of the professor whom he idolized while a college student. The social changes in the decades that followed his departure from Columbia were to have only "cosmetic" effects on his outward behavior; his acceptance of these principles about human nature and man's role in society was never really to waver. Of course, there was one more tidbit of wisdom that Wouk may well have learned from Edman, a bit of practical philosophy that would give a would-be writer the material wherewithal to enjoy the good life that the Columbia University philosopher described in such passionate detail: "As for the respectable bourgeois rabble whom our sophisticated despise, these comfortable bumpkins cannot get enough of the traditional simple virtues and simple souls. Write them a story, as an Englishman did recently, of a brave father come down in the world, fighting the good fight against slimy obstacles for the love of his pure and devoted son, and you will have hundreds of thousands at your feet and at your publisher's" (Edman 1929, 207).[26] From the publication of *Aurora Dawn* through the war novels and the accounts of the Jewish experience in America, Wouk never forgot that bit of advice. Always with an eye on the popular reading public, he turned out novels with strong narrative lines, stories in which the general reader—that "comfortable bumpkin" in which Edman had such faith—would find comfort, solace—and a good night's reading. In that fact lie both Wouk's strength, and most of his weaknesses.

Chapter Two

Apprenticeship in Fiction and Drama

Aurora Dawn

Despite the continual threat of danger and the myriad duties involved in keeping a fighting ship afloat and ready for combat, men at sea—even during wartime—have always found themselves with time on their hands. Herman Wouk was no exception, but instead of engaging in card games and conversation, he spent much of his time aboard USS *Zane* reading and writing. In July 1943, at Tulagi in the Solomon Islands, he began drafting a play based on his prewar experience of commercial radio. For several months he toiled over the dialogue, until in October of that year he decided to transform the story into a novel.[1] Perhaps the change to fiction was inspired by the many novels he was reading: Dickens and Cervantes were constant companions during the long hours when he was off watch. The influence of eighteenth-century masters such as Fielding and Smollett is quite evident in the final version of this story of Madison Avenue radio advertising, which was the outcome of Wouk's leisure activity.

The manuscript continued to grow, albeit slowly, during the remaining years of Wouk's naval service; he completed the first part by 1945, and finished the manuscript after his release from active service in 1946.[2] Shrewdly, before he had completed the work, he sent initial chapters to his mentor Irwin Edman, who had connections with New York publishers. Edman managed to get someone at Simon & Schuster to read the draft Wouk had sent him, and the editor was impressed enough to recommend the work for publication. Not surprisingly, the book is dedicated to Edman.

Wouk delivered the finished manuscript in May 1946, and Simon & Schuster brought out a modest run in 1947. Then, good fortune struck—the first of many strokes of luck—when the Book-of-the-Month Club chose *Aurora Dawn* as a monthly selection. Such widespread publicity helped make the book a minor commercial success; even more importantly, perhaps, it guaranteed Wouk ready entrée to publishers when he completed his second novel some time later.

The subject of this first novel is the advertising industry. Relying on his inside knowledge of radio program production, Wouk created a fable about a young advertising executive, Andrew Reale. Reale, in love with the beautiful Honey Beaton, finds his fidelity challenged by the equally beautiful Carol Marquis—who happens to be the daughter of business magnate Talmadge Marquis. Things become complicated when Reale finds that he must conduct an advertising campaign to promote Marquis's product, Aurora Dawn soap. The novel traces Andrew's struggles to choose one woman over the other—clearly a dilemma intended to symbolize the choice between differing value systems—while he goes about the business of promoting Aurora Dawn, thereby increasing the radio station's revenues. Wouk gives the story an extra twist by sending Andrew off to convince the Reverend Calvin Stanfield, a backwoods evangelist, to bring his brand of spirituality to the radio. In Stanfield, the radio moguls see a means of increasing the station's audience share, and thereby attracting more advertising revenues. Reale comes to realize that what Stanfield preaches is an alternative to the fast-lane lifestyle represented by figures such as Talmadge and Carol Marquis, or the painter Mike Wilde, whose presence in the novel also represents the decadence of modern art. Fortunately, all ends well for Wouk's first hero; Reale chooses the right wife, and he retires from radio advertising to take up a life in the West.

No doubt Wouk had significant firsthand experience on which to draw for both plot and characterization in this inaugural work. Even before he went to work for Fred Allen, he would surely have been familiar with the comedian's popular "Linit Bath Club Review," begun in 1932; while working for Allen on the immensely popular "Sal Hypatica Review" show, sponsored by Bristol Meyers, he became an expert in the backstage maneuverings of the radio advertising business.[3] The idea for a character such as Dr. Stanfield may have come from observing similar figures featured in the "Walking Down Main Street" section of Allen's radio show. Nonetheless, the characters seem so overdrawn and stereotypical that one is tempted to look beyond the realm of personal experience for Wouk's models.

As Diana Trilling observed in her review of the novel, *Aurora Dawn* is, like so many other works appearing immediately after the close of World War II, "heavy with portent and pretension."[4] The slight, humorous account of Andrew Reale's attempts to make it big in the advertising world is laden with moralistic overtones, suggesting—at times heavy-handedly—that the hero is a young Everyman, similar to such eighteenth-century figures as Joseph Andrews and Tom Jones.[5] Wouk's narrative devices underline his reliance on that novelistic tradition. Though of modest length, the novel is divided into two parts and 27 chapters. Each chapter is preceded by a brief summation of the action, written in the style of Fielding. An example gives a good sense of this method. "Chapter SEVEN: In which the reader has the privilege of meeting Talmadge Marquis, reigning satrap in the industrial realm of Soap, and learns more of the truly fascinating history of Aurora Dawn; but which he may skip if he is only following the love story." The entry for Chapter 3 remarks on the "very sound reflections" of the narrator, who speaks frequently to readers in a rather chummy fashion (in the manner of Fielding, Dickens, or Trollope), confiding secrets about characters' behavior and motivations and reminding them that this is, after all, a story. The authorial interjections and digressions, and the repeated suggestions to readers on how to respond, recalls an antiquated a tradition of novel-writing—something Wouk acknowledges in his Preface to the 1983 Pocket Books edition. "By instinct," he reports retrospectively, "I was getting as far as I could from current fashions in writing."[6]

Most critical commentary focused on two aspects of the novel: Wouk's style and his intrusive narrator. Wouk's "instinct" to revert to older narrative forms received mixed reviews. Spencer Klaw thought Wouk had "put to excellent use the manner of his eighteenth-century masters in satire," but in her critique of the novel for *Kirkus* Diana Trilling found this attempt to tell a modern story in a Victorian framework "forced" and "artificial"; in a second, separate review Trilling dismissed the eighteenth-century "affectations" as "pretentious and imitative."[7] Mark Charney observed that the extremely stylized presentation adversely affected Wouk's ability to make a point in his narrative.[8] Though *Booklist*'s reviewer took pleasure in reading a novel that "happily avoids vulgar language and crude love passages," Trilling noted that there was almost universal objection among reviewers to the publisher's claims that Wouk had "rescued the beautiful English language" from the barbarism of Hemingway and "restored it to the tradition of Fielding."[9] While Klaw judged the work "a delightfully fresh and funny satire . . . that never descends to mere burlesque," and the *Saturday Review*'s Percy Atkinson had praise for Wouk's "good-natured banter and philosophic discursiveness," another reviewer judged the work "an almost unbearably arch story."[10]

Commentary on Wouk's use of the intrusive narrator is equally divided. Klaw thought Wouk succeeded admirably in creating both engaging characters and a narrator whose "mock gravity" captures readers' attention and amuses them while making serious (though not overly serious) observations on modern society (Klaw, 3). The "engaging chatter" of the narrator, another reviewer noted, keeps readers continuously amused and entertained and forms a bond of companionship that allows Wouk to expose the inner workings of the advertising industry—and its foibles—effortlessly and convincingly (Atkinson, 17). What the novel lacks, however, is a sense of genuine empathy for both its characters and the world in which they live. Trilling notes that Wouk seems to want to keep "a moral distance between himself and his subject" (*Nation*, 636)— to be expected, perhaps, from a writer of satiric fiction, but justifiable only when the author can evoke through satire his own moral vision. That vision seems lacking in *Aurora Dawn*, and its absence forces the critical reader to regard the novel as little more than a divertissement.

Despite harsh reviews, a large readership often builds a writer's confidence, and Wouk's faith in his abilities as a novelist increased. Shortly after *Aurora Dawn* appeared, he published an article in *'47: The Magazine of the Year*, in which he bids farewell to the world of gag writing. Titled "Make It with Kissing," the piece outlines Wouk's reasons for abandoning the anonymous backstages of radio and television stations for the popular novelist's limelight.

About this same time, Wouk met the highly successful agent Harold Matson, who convinced him that, now that he was a Book-of-the-Month Club author, he could strike a better deal for his second novel than the agreement from Simon & Schuster for *Aurora Dawn*. The idea must have appealed to Wouk, because he signed on with Matson, who handled his literary matters for several years. In fact, Wouk consulted Matson about doing a movie script based on the Navy's weather reconnaissance units. The idea of doing something about the Navy had been suggested to Wouk by a Navy man he met in late 1947. Wouk actually composed a short outline for such a movie—eventually produced under the title *Slattery's Hurricane*—and though he did not write the script, he composed an expanded treatment of the idea (12 pages) and then went to California (at $300 a week plus expenses and a $5,000 option) to prepare a screen treatment.[11]

City Boy

Wouk may have been tempted by the movies, but he was determined to make his mark as a novelist. The ink was hardly dry on the printed pages of *Aurora Dawn* when Wouk began work on a second manuscript. For his subject, he turned to his childhood memories, as the son of immigrant Jewish parents in New York City, threads that he would weave into *City Boy: The Adventures of Herbie Bookbinder*. Like Wouk, Herbie Bookbinder is the favored son of Jewish parents who want a better life for him in America than they had in the old country. Like Wouk's father, Herbie's father runs a laundry in New York City, and uses his hard-earned profits to buy his children the best of everything: food, clothes, and (of course) the opportunity to attend summer camp in the Berkshires.

The central action of the novel concerns Herbie's pursuit of his first love, Lucille Glass, as well as his preparations for, and attendance at, summer camp. The romance of attending such a camp—and having Lucille close by—appears to be almost beyond the 12-year-old's belief; but Wouk's portrait of the camp, run by the school principal (the Quilp-like Mr. Gauss) is far from idyllic. Much of the novel's humor comes from Herbie's idealistic representations of his squalid environment. There is a serious side to the work, however. A series of misadventures at camp leads to Herbie's departure from the Berkshires and return to New York, to obtain money from his father. While sneaking into the laundry, he uncovers a plot by his father's associates to ruin the family business. Naturally, Herbie reveals the plot and saves the family; all's well that ends well in the world of preteen romance.

An early reviewer, noting that Wouk's "sharp, lighthearted picture of public school life in the Bronx" is particularly accurate, suggests that the immediacy of the book's impact comes from Wouk's ability to write "from memory" about these events.[12] Nevertheless, while the plot and setting may come from Wouk's autobiography, there is little question that the primary sources for Wouk's portrait of American youth are the novels of Mark Twain and, to a lesser extent, Booth Tarkington's Penrod stories. Like Tom Sawyer, Herbie is captivated by his own Becky Thatcher, the winsome Lucille Glass, and much of his activity is motivated by his desire to make himself acceptable to her as a hero—just as one might expect from a 12-year-old, whose ideas of love and adulthood are shaped as much from romantic literature and adolescent rumor, as they are from more adult sources. With some justification, the *Herald*

Tribune captioned its review of the novel "Don Quixote from the Bronx" (Sugrue, 4).

A contemporary reviewer called the novel "a tragicomedy of youngsters," with "no profound social significance or jibes at modern mores."[13] Herbie's story—clearly an adventure motivated in part by puppy love— certainly makes for entertaining reading, and it is one of Wouk's few books (besides *The Caine Mutiny*) that continued to attract readers for years after publication.[14] In it, Wouk demonstrates his ability to carry his readers along on an adventure, and even critics who panned the work often found themselves acknowledging the novelist's "ability to tell a story," his "fine eye for living detail," and his "enormous sympathy for his fellow beings."[15]

The novel did not achieve the immediate commercial success of its predecessor, however. Sales were sluggish, prompted perhaps by the absence of readers' interest in the subject of adolescence in the years immediately following World War II, and by early reviews which were more critical than laudatory. A few observers, such as Marc Brandel in the *New York Times*, thought Wouk's recreation of the days before the Depression and World War II made "delightful reading."[16] The majority sided with Richard Gelman, who judged the novel "a complete failure" (Gelman, 10).

Trying Theater: *The Traitor*

During the months following completion of *City Boy*, Wouk's attention turned once again to the theater. Perhaps inspired by the success of *Slattery's Hurricane*, or stung by the failure of *City Boy* to repeat the success of *Aurora Dawn*, Wouk sought the medium of drama to express his ideas on a subject of growing importance to both himself and his countrymen: communism. The result was the 1949 production of *The Traitor*, a melodrama centering on the moral crisis in the life of philosophy professor Tobias Emanuel. Emanuel learns that a favorite former student, the young American physicist Allen Carr, is about to turn over the secret of the atomic bomb to Russian agents. Though Emanuel has always been a liberal, the thought of the Communists gaining such a weapon is too much for him. Emanuel manages to convince Carr to abandon his plan and participate in a scheme to capture the Communist spies; with the help of Navy intelligence, they are successful. But their effort has its price; Carr is killed in the climactic scene of the drama, though in his deathbed address to the audience he makes an eloquent plea for cooperation between the superpowers.

The play opened on Broadway at the Forty-Eighth Street Theater on 31 March 1949, and ran for 67 performances—hardly a smashing success by theatrical standards. Even more than the novelist, the playwright depends on reviews for the commercial success of his effort, and criticism of Wouk's drama was rather harsh. The highest praise it garnered was as a "thriller" which dealt with "topical" issues sure to lure the public into the theater.[17] The critic for *Newsweek* judged it a "promising first try," which, though "too talky," manages to "come very much to the point on an urgent and topical theme."[18] In the *Saturday Review*, John Mason Brown praised the play as a "tense piece of theater"—"once it really starts moving."[19]

Wouk attributed the short run to bad luck. "My wife and I went to the theater [on opening night] . . . already planning how we would spend the money. Monday I called [the director, who said,] 'It's a big hit . . . but nobody's coming. There's a taxi strike on.' "[20] That reasoning is amusing, but perhaps disingenuous. *The Traitor* lacks dramatic interest. Too much of the dialogue consists of harangues, in which characters become mouthpieces for different ideologies; the audience is certainly less concerned with them as people, than with choosing the side of the good guys against the evil communist empire. The heavy-handed portrait of Soviet agents makes for little dramatic conflict, and the protagonist's change of heart in the final act, when he decides not to betray his country, seems completely out-of-character.[21]

The Traitor shares certain weaknesses with much of Wouk's early work. While he exhibits exceptional storytelling gifts, when he sees an opportunity to declaim conservative values, he abandons all pretense of fiction and launches into rhetoric, using whatever character is at hand to bring home his point. I would not argue that Wouk is wrong to promote conservative values, as some of his harsher critics have maintained. But as Henry James reminds us, in "The Art of Fiction," "We must grant the artist his subject matter, his donée"—and then we must judge him by what he makes of it. In these first two novels and in his first Broadway play, Wouk scores high marks for description and in most instances for plot. When he wanders away from the popular art of storytelling and into the realm of serious debate, he begins to falter. In none of these three works is he fully successful in subordinating ideas to action and description; he simply does not let his story reveal his theme.

But the apprenticeship had its value, for from it Wouk learned several things. He was good at writing about worlds he knew well: he could make characters come alive and scenes appear real when he focused on familiar territory and circumstances. Furthermore, he felt that he had something to say to his fellow citizens about the society in which they lived, and he could say it best through the medium of fiction. He could win a large audience if he emulated the comfortable narrative style of the eighteenth- and nineteenth-century masters who so appealed to him. And finally, he could influence that audience to accept his values—or reinforce values already held by that audience—through his writings, while making a comfortable living. Small wonder that, after only three short years, the politically conservative popular novelist emerged from the gag writer of the 1930s. How popular, and how conservative, was to be proven by his next novel.

Chapter Three

Becoming a Best-Selling Author: *The Caine Mutiny*

Writing about War at Sea

Perhaps it was his success in drawing upon childhood memories for *City Boy* or upon his experience in radio for *Aurora Dawn* that prompted Wouk to draw upon other events in his life for his third novel. Shortly after Pearl Harbor, Wouk had managed to join the Navy. After attending midshipman school at Columbia University and communications school in Annapolis, he was assigned to a destroyer-minesweeper, USS *Zane*, in the Pacific. He spent three years at sea, participating in several historic military campaigns. While he had no intention of remaining in the service when the war ended, Wouk did find his military experience rewarding, and he developed a lifelong appreciation for the navy.[1]

The Caine Mutiny was begun in 1949, while Wouk (who had remained in the naval reserve) was on a training cruise aboard USS *Saipan*.[2] Much of the background for the story is undoubtedly drawn from Wouk's recollections of navy life during World War II. Having served aboard destroyer-minesweepers, Wouk was intimately familiar with their workings, and could describe in detail the mechanics of maneuvering, supplying, and managing such vessels. Like several of the novel's fictional officers, he had held various posts of increasing responsibility, rising to the position of executive officer aboard USS *Southard*.

In a short note that serves as a preface to the novel, Wouk is careful to point out that "this is a work of fiction," and that no mutiny like the one he describes has ever happened in the United States Navy.[3] Nevertheless, his longtime friend Arnold Beichman notes that as early as 1945 the novelist was deeply concerned with a problem that he saw during the war: the tension between regular navy men who had chosen a service career long before the outbreak of hostilities, and reservists who joined the navy from various walks of life when the country needed them in a time of crisis. Wouk noted in a memorandum to his superiors that junior officers often swapped "Captain Bligh" stories about particularly harsh commanders; he thought the navy needed to pay more attention to the ideas and suggestions of junior officers who found themselves forced to give up many of their democratic freedoms when they joined the service.[4] The role of the citizen/sailor lies at the center of Wouk's complex novel, but is not its only theme.

In many ways, *The Caine Mutiny* displays Wouk's progress as a novelist. His previous novels had been of modest length, and were heavily indebted to literary predecessors. One definite advance in this work is the increased complexity of both action and theme. F. I. Carpenter, one of Wouk's early academic critics, observed that in *The Caine Mutiny* "the skeleton of allegory which distorted Wouk's earlier novels now becomes fully fleshed in living characters." The work is, in Carpenter's judgment, "a straightforward, realistic novel in the tradition of W. D. Howells and Sinclair Lewis."[5] Even a critic hostile to Wouk admitted that *The Caine Mutiny* was "the most influential of the war novels posing an ethical problem."[6]

A contemporary praised Wouk as "an exceptionally good storyteller" who handles the adventures of his hero, Willie Keith, "with a directness and a swiftness that bear the mark of the practiced professional writer."[7] Another reviewer described the novel as "a skillfully written, modest, and occasionally gripping story about the American Navy in the last war."[8] Such summaries hardly do the work justice. *The Caine Mutiny* is actually a carefully structured novel, following the model of the bildungsroman; it is, in its largest sense, the education of Willie Keith, who changes from spoiled rich adolescent to worldly wise, battle-hardened adult. Of course, it is not unusual to find the combination of war novel and bildungsroman in a single work, since it is a commonplace that young men sent off to war often grow up as a result of their experiences. However, the lessons Willie learns about himself and about the nature of military society make *The Caine Mutiny* unusual among war novels.

Wouk divides the novel into seven large sections, each marking a stage in Willie's maturation. The first opens in 1942, in the aftermath of Pearl Harbor. The young Princeton graduate Willie Keith leaves his wealthy family, which is dominated by his doting mother, to enlist in the navy and attend officer candidate school at Columbia. The world of the navy seems to Willie much like the fantasy world Alice encounters in Wonderland, a comparison that Wouk makes explicit by titling his first chapter "Through the Looking Glass." Willie's first adventures in this bureaucratic wonderland are more like nightmares: a series of mishaps results in his accumulating almost the maximum number of demerits for expulsion. He spends most of his time at Columbia trying to learn the navy ways, simply to prove that he has the mettle to stand on his own, without the significant prop of his mother. At the same time, this section introduces readers to Willie's love life, in the person of "May Wynn"— also known as Marie Minotti, a singer who works at a nightclub where Willie plays piano before he makes his momentous decision to join the service.

Willie survives officer candidate school, but seems not to have fully understood the nature of navy life, and the sacrifices he will be required to make. He is pained when, instead of being assigned to a staff billet in the States, he receives orders for USS *Caine*, a World War I destroyer convert- ed for minesweeping duty in this latest worldwide conflagration. With a heavy heart, Willie departs for Pearl Harbor and the Pacific theater.

Part two focuses on Willie's first months aboard the *Caine*, when he learns to hate the slovenly Captain DeVriess—and gets into further trouble when, in the excitement of a demanding exercise at sea, he fails to deliver an important message to the captain. This section introduces several characters who will play important roles. Among the most important is Steve Maryk, who becomes the ship's executive officer later in the war. Another is Tom Keefer, Willie's first boss aboard the *Caine*, and later executive officer and commander of the ship.

In section three, Wouk completes the cast of principals who will play out the shipboard drama at the novel's center. Philip Francis Queeg, lieutenant commander in the regular navy, an Annapolis graduate who is by his own account a "book man" who follows regulations explicitly, relieves DeVriess as captain of the *Caine*. For most of this and the fol- lowing two sections, Wouk traces the growing estrangement between Queeg and his officers and crew. In a series of episodes, Queeg displays qualities totally unbecoming to an officer and which certainly make his fitness for command highly questionable. Some examples are worth not- ing. In his first attempt to conn (i.e., to maneuver) his ship out of the harbor, he grazes another ship and then runs aground. At another time, he explodes when he sees a sailor whose shirttail is hanging, and while berating him he allows the ship to turn full circle, cutting a cable attached to an expensive target the *Caine* is towing. Before the ship returns to San Francisco for much-needed repairs, Queeg collects ration coupons for purchasing alcoholic beverages from his officers and illegally transports a huge quantity of liquor to the States. When he loses his cache because the lead-lined case in which he has hidden the bottles sinks in Oakland harbor, he blames Willie for the loss, since Willie is officer-in-charge of the small boat which is to smuggle Queeg's liquor ashore. As these events occur, the officers and men who were initially quite favorably disposed toward their new captain grow to despise him; only Maryk, who ascends to the position of executive officer, remains loyal and refuses to listen to criticism.

Worse is still to come, however. In the first wartime engagement under Queeg's command, the *Caine* speeds ahead of the small boats it is to escort to a beachhead, leaving behind a yellow dye indicating the position from which these boats should begin their shore assault. In that same engagement, Willie notices that Queeg always positions himself on the side of the bridge (the ship's main command center), away from the enemy guns which deliver fire at the approaching destroyer. Later, Queeg retaliates for a small infraction by denying the crew water for days. When the remains of a gallon of strawberries (one of his favorite foods) is stolen from the officers' wardroom, he instigates a ship-wide search for a key to the wardroom locker in an attempt to find the thief. Even when he is told that there is no key, and that the real culprits have been identified, he continues the search.

Actions such as these finally convince Steve Maryk that Queeg may indeed be unfit for command. Spurred on by Tom Keefer, who remarks upon the parallels between Queeg's actions and the personality traits of a psychotic, Maryk begins to keep a log of Queeg's strange behavior. The climax of part five is the actual mutiny, which occurs at the height of a typhoon. Queeg appears incapable of guiding the ship rationally, so Maryk steps in to assume command.

Throughout these episodes, Willie Keith stands close to the center of the action. Once a favorite of Queeg, he soon becomes the captain's whipping boy, and the recipient of his threats. When Maryk relieves Queeg, Willie is on duty, and he must make the crucial decision to either obey Maryk's commands or remain loyal to his captain. Willie chooses to side with the executive officer, and hence becomes a mutineer.

Part six, "The Court-Martial," recounts the navy's prosecution of those who actively defied the *Caine*'s duly-appointed captain. In perhaps the novel's most overtly dramatic section, these chapters relate the court-martial procedures in detail. During the trial, a brilliant young Jewish lawyer, Lieutenant Barney Greenwald, manages to discredit the navy psychologists who testify to Queeg's sanity and to destroy Queeg himself when the captain takes the stand. The jubilation of the mutineers, who are acquitted as a result of Greenwald's histrionics, is short-

lived, however. At their victory party, the lawyer castigates them bitterly for forcing him to destroy Queeg, and he lays the blame for the
mutiny squarely at the feet of Tom Keefer, whose behind-the-scenes
maneuvering and intellectual disdain for navy bureaucracy prodded
Maryk, Keith, and the others to more direct action.

The novel's final section, "The Last Captain of the *Caine*," serves as a
kind of epilogue. Tom Keefer, how captain of the ship, behaves in much
the same manner as Queeg; when the *Caine* is hit by a Japanese
kamikaze, Keefer jumps ship, clutching the manuscript of a novel he has
been writing about his experiences in the navy. Willie is forced into heroic action to save the vessel. The trial, and the events leading up to it,
have seasoned Willie in many ways. He makes a decision to take up his
romance with May/Marie, despite his mother's disapproval. The final
chapter finds him assuming command of the *Caine* and bringing the ship
back to the United States where it will be dismantled into scrap.

The Novel's Popularity

The Caine Mutiny unquestionably earned Wouk a prominent place
among American popular authors. The reasons for that achievement are
complex, and they also offer a partial explanation for Wouk's castigation
by the academic community. The immense commercial success that
Wouk's book has enjoyed since its appearance in 1951, however, cannot
be denied.

"Timing is all," to paraphrase Shakespeare, and the appearance of
Wouk's novel coincided with a moment when the reading public, fresh
from experiencing the horrors of World War II directly or through
graphic newspaper and newsreel accounts, was ready to see that conflict
turned into exciting entertainment. As Albert Van Nostrand observed,
"the normal war novel" has been a "most familiar species of contemporary American fiction" for some time, "partly the result of a widespread
obsession for authenticity which the subject itself inspires, and partly the
result of the stylizing of certain fictional conventions" (Van Nostrand,
182). *The Caine Mutiny* was one of a number of novels that took for their
subject the great global conflagration that had changed the world:
Norman Mailer's *The Naked and the Dead* (1948), James Gould Cozzens's
Guard of Honor (1948), and James Jones's *From Here to Eternity* (1951)
headed a long list of fictional accounts that dealt with every aspect of the
war, from platoon combat to global strategy. Predictably, dozens of these
works never made it past the first edition. Several, including Wouk's

novel, have achieved lasting popularity and have remained in print to engage the interests of generations who have only a historical or antiquarian interest in World War II.

In some ways, however, *The Caine Mutiny* has transcended its genre. As early as 1956, F. I. Carpenter prophesied that *The Caine Mutiny* "may well become the most successful novel published in the twentieth century" (Carpenter, 212). The numbers bear out Carpenter's prediction. In November 1951, 62,491 copies were sold—"more . . . than many 'best selling' novels do in their entire careers."[9] The trade edition sold over 200,000 copies in the first nine months after publication. By the end of 1952, that number had doubled. Additionally, *The Caine Mutiny* was offered as a selection by the Book-of-the-Month Club, the Literary Guild, the People's Book Club, and the Doubleday Dollar Book Club. It was condensed in *Reader's Digest*, and serialized in 45 newspapers (Van Nostrand, 194). Twenty-three months after publication, sales were over the one-million mark, with purchases ranging between 2,000 and 3,000 a week. The novel held first place on the *New York Times* and the *New York Herald Tribune* best-seller lists from August 1951 to August 1952 (McClean, 194). Before the end of the decade, domestic sales had risen to over 3,000,000, and the book had been translated into 16 languages.[10] Certainly Carpenter cannot be far wrong in his assessment.

The reasons for the immediate and continuing popularity of *The Caine Mutiny* are varied. Some are practical. For years, there was great interest in the novel in both high schools and colleges.[11] The book could be "easily understood," one teacher and scholar noted, and so "the student is freed from complexity of style or meaning to examine the novel from a technical point of view" (Haley, 71).

Further support came from another source. As early as 1953, the navy was recommending the novel as "collateral reading" in its officer candidate schools (McClean, 194). When the United States Naval Academy introduced an elective program in English in the mid-1970s, *The Caine Mutiny* and *The Caine Mutiny Court-Martial* appeared in the syllabus of the academy's "Literature of the Sea" elective, and was sometimes required reading in sections of the freshman composition course (especially those taught by military officers). The movie version has been a staple in the professional development program for years.[12]

Such a limited audience alone could not make any work a national best-seller, nor could it guarantee lasting success. Obviously, the reasons for Wouk's success lay beyond his appeal to those interested in naval operations. One explanation for his wide reading public is his ability to tell a story directly, simply, and swiftly, avoiding the danger of getting mired in philosophical inquiry. Nevertheless, Spencer Brown observed that "Wouk's huge sales are due, I am sure, not wholly to his narrative power but partly to his introduction of great moral issues."[13] This was not the first appearance of a moral dimension in Wouk's work. There is "a persistent but disguised moralism in all Wouk's fiction," F. I. Carpenter noted, but *The Caine Mutiny* ranks above Wouk's other works "because it is the least moralistic" (Carpenter, 215)—that is, it speaks less directly to the reader about moral issues than did Wouk's earlier novels and plays.

Though the majority of reviewers were highly critical of Wouk for the conservative stance he takes at the end of the novel, the general public seemed to value his approach. The "middle-class readers" who make up the majority of book-buyers in the United States responded enthusiastically to Wouk's defense of the navy; they did not find the castigation of Keefer and leftist intellectuals confusing in any way. In fact, as William H. Whyte noted of early readers of *The Caine Mutiny*, "most people got the point—and most of them agreed with it."[14] Millions of buyers would probably have agreed with Whyte, who felt that readers "must, with the author, make a choice, and a choice that is presented as an ultimately moral one." The "boldness" with which Wouk asserts conservative values makes *The Caine Mutiny* "something of a landmark in the shift of American values" (Whyte, 243).

According to Lydia McClean, the early success of the novel was "largely due to the fact that the people who read it like[d] it and recommend[ed] it to other people" (McClean, 294). Word-of-mouth advertising is often the best kind of recommendation, even in an age of media hype; a lesson Wouk had learned as early as 1947, when he lampooned advertising practices in *Aurora Dawn*. No one had to convince him that his best source of publicity would be avid readers—no matter what the critics had to say.

Sources and Themes

If the eighteenth-century comic masters were the models for *Aurora Dawn*, and Mark Twain the guide for *City Boy*, then certainly Joseph Conrad and Herman Melville are the literary precursors of *The Caine Mutiny*. There are echoes of *The Nigger of the "Narcissus"* and *Billy Budd* in Wouk's account of the mutiny and trial. Many of the characters are like those in the sea tales of these two novelists. F. I. Carpenter suggests that in *The Caine Mutiny* Wouk reverses the situation Melville presents in *Billy Budd*, making Queeg an incompetent commander, whereas Melville's Vere is exemplary (Carpenter, 212).[15] There are parallels between Wouk's characters and the captain in Conrad's "Secret Sharer," for example, or even the hero of *Lord Jim*. As critic Peter Jones succinctly noted, "Conrad is behind many scenes in *The Caine Mutiny*. The double, Tom-Roland Keefer; Tom Keefer's dumb refusal to act when he should, and his eloquent leap, with his rueful self-analysis, and above all, the merging of that austere code of the necessary and man's struggle to cope with it—all evoke the atmosphere of Conrad's tales, but with a comic diffidence."[16] Following the lead of Conrad and other writers of sea tales, Wouk uses his specific locale both to concentrate action and, simultaneously, to suggest the universal significance of the events he recounts. "Like Conrad," Jones says, "Wouk uses a ship for background and unity—here a small warship. It is an ideal setting: there is no escape from incessant contact with men under constant duress, no relief from or for the man who commands" (Jones, 74).

The Caine Mutiny has been described as "a blend of popular entertainment and 'serious' moralizing."[17] The book is neither "stark realism" nor "escapism," the reviewer for *Catholic World* concluded: instead, in the novel Wouk "attempts intellectual insight into the experience" he records. "The result is, in the strict and proper sense of the term, a comic view of the war."[18] Beneath the surface of this fast-paced adventure novel, Wouk deals simultaneously with several themes. The focus on Willie Keith suggests that this novel is primarily concerned with the process of maturation.[19] That growth operates on two levels: we see Willie Keith, the spoiled young aristocrat, become a mature adult. At the same time, Willie serves as a metaphor for his country, which also matures as a result of World War II. His "transformation" is "intended an as allegory of America's own 'coming of age'," says W. J. Stuckey, who believes Wouk's main point is to show that maturity consists in "a willingness blindly to follow authority wherever it may lead" (Stuckey, 163). Though I disagree with Stuckey about the dependence of either Willie's—or America's—maturity on blind, unthinking obedience, their maturations seems clearly linked. Willie's father makes the comparison explicit, in his deathbed letter that Willie opens while on his way to join the crew of the *Caine*. "It seems to me," he writes to his son, "that you're very much like our country—young, naive, spoiled"—but with the indomitable spirit to carry on the pioneer tradition that allowed the group of immigrants who had come to the Western Hemisphere to make a better life for themselves (*CM*, 64). Just as the novel presents "a crisis of moral responsibility" for its central character (Van Nostrand, 200), it also explores America's moral crisis in dealing with Hitler and the problem of the Holocaust. In neither instance is the protagonist fully absolved of guilt.

I am inclined to side with Rhoda Metraux, who sees Willie's growth in more conventional terms. She suggests that the novel is "the story of the making of a man. Willie Keith is taken from the world of his mother and re-made into the son of his father in the masculine world of the *Caine* . . . in its telling Wouk redefines one of our most firmly held beliefs—in a man's right to rebel."[20] The significance of the theme is made apparent by Wouk himself: "The story begins with Willie Keith because the event turned on his personality as the massive door of a vault turns on a small jewel bearing" (*CM*, v). The events that mark his career from midshipman to captain of the *Caine* are a series of decisions that help him grow in self-confidence and self-knowledge. "Everyone's life pivots on one or two moments" (*CM*, 501), Keefer tells Willie after the court-martial, when they have just suffered a kamikaze attack during which Keefer showed cowardice and Willie exceptional heroism (*CM*, 501).

Like many bildungsromans, the story of Willie Keith is the tale of a young man's search for a father—and his own transformation into a father-figure. Willie's father, dominated by a wife whose wealth has made him comfortable but whose social status has kept him from fulfilling his dream of contributing to society through medical research, is pleased to see his son enter the service in a great cause (*CM*, 64).[21] Like his father, Willie has dreams—he wants to spend his life in Dickens scholarship (*CM*, 18)—but the threat of being drafted drives him to seek a commission in the navy. Though his motives are not necessarily noble, his actions put him in circumstances that will allow him to achieve psychological independence from both his parents.[22]

Throughout his naval career, Willie confronts a series of father-figures: Ensigns Brain and Acres at midshipmen's school; the kindly admiral who likes his piano playing and offers to keep him safely away from the fighting; his first skipper aboard the *Caine*, Captain DeVriess; senior officers aboard the destroyer-minesweeper, Steve Maryk and Tom Keefer; and of course, Captain Queeg. The title for the novel's first section, "Through the Looking Glass," with its overt reference to Lewis Carroll, suggests the extreme difference between the bizarre world of the navy and the world Willie knew before he enlisted.[23] Willie must learn to measure up to standards he did not create, to gain the approval of his "father," and eventually, to become a father to those serving under him. Readers may lose sight of Willie's progress toward adulthood amid the tumultuous events aboard ship, but there are subtle signs. The rebellious boy balks at touring the entire ship, including the crow's nest, with Harding, the other new arrival (*CM*, 80–81), and at drawing a sketch of the ship before he is permitted to go ashore (*CM*, 83–90). A year later, however, Willie conducts rigorous training for new ensigns Jorgenson and Duceley, finally having understood that the harsh regimen he had been forced to follow has its value, even if those subjected to it cannot see its sense. (*CM*, 240–43). Similarly, early in his career aboard the *Caine*, while watching the crew recover minesweeping equipment, in the excitement of the moment he forgets that he has received an important official message; fortunately, Captain DeVriess reprimands him, but in a way that does not break his spirit (*CM*, 120). Much later, after he has assumed the mantle of authority that DeVriess, Queeg, Maryk, White, and Keefer have worn before him, he comes to understand the awesome responsibility that comes with command of a major combat vessel (*CM*, 520).

We can even see Willie's attitude toward deprivation and hard work changing as his time aboard the *Caine* lengthens. The newly arrived Ensign Keith complains bitterly about the amount of work he is expected to do, and the harsh treatment to which he is subjected under DeVriess (*CM*, 91–93). Yet he learns to bear up under the harsher, nonsensical demands Queeg makes, by reminding himself that he is an officer, who does not need to cry to anyone when things get tough (*CM*, 278). During the notorious "strawberry" incident, when Queeg orders his officers to conduct a top-to-bottom search of the ship for the locker key he is sure has been stolen, Willie takes one of the new ensigns aside and assures him that, though the skipper's orders seem strange, they must dutifully comply if good order is to be maintained (*CM*, 331). Some might find this behavior reminiscent of a mindless martinet; yet Willie has not been deceived by the captain or by the system. He is only putting aside individual concerns for the greater good of maintaining a system that must be preserved in its larger context, if the American forces are to win against their enemies. He trusts that, at the proper time and in the proper place, he and the other officers aboard ship can deal with Queeg in a way that does not endanger themselves or the crew. Only when he sees Queeg's inability to function in the height of the typhoon, and the imminent danger posed to the ship and crew by the captain's temporary paralysis, does he act in an overtly disloyal manner.

Willie learns to perform admirably under pressure; his ability to do so is best exemplified during the typhoon, when he assures the crew that they are in capable hands and that they will get through the storm if they simply follow orders (*CM*, 364). Later, when the *Caine* returns to sea after Maryk and Keith are acquitted of mutiny, Willie acts heroically to save the ship when it is damaged by a kamikaze pilot (*CM*, 493). Reflecting on his actions, Tom Keefer—who has distinguished himself by his cowardly jump into the sea, clutching the manuscript of his novel—remarks to Willie about how much he has changed in the two years he has served aboard the jinxed destroyer-minesweeper. Keefer reveals to Willie that, when Willie first reported aboard the *Caine*, DeVriess predicted the young ensign would be an outstanding officer (*CM*, 500). Willie's actions in the face of hard times, unfair treatment, and great personal strain have proved DeVriess right. Though he feels a great sense of relief that he has lived through the war, Willie is also saddened when the news of surrender arrives; he muses that peace seems to have robbed him of the chance to command the ship on which he has undergone so many travails (*CM*, 513). Keefer receives notice of his discharge, however, before the ship is sent to the salvage yard, and Willie is tapped to skipper the ship on her last voyage to the junkheap. There is irony in this, certainly, but the fact that the *Caine* is sailing back to America to be scrapped does not diminish the significance of Willie's assumption of command. He has become the father-figure, serving as the last captain of the destroyer-minesweeper: sailors now refer to him as "the old man," a term of respect in military circles.[24]

The reader expects that Willie's maturation process will extend to his love life as well. That demand probably explains the presence of May Wynn in the story, but the account of Willie's romance with the young Italian singer has generally received lukewarm responses from both reviewers and readers. Mark Charney considers the "consistently sentimental, shallow romance between Keith and May Wynn" the "novel's only notable fault."[25] Lee Rogow judges it "regrettably jejune."[26] No doubt Wouk wants to show that Willie is capable of replacing his mother with a woman of his own choice. Unfortunately, the scenes between the two lovers are filled with stilted dialogue, and neither of their actions appear sufficiently motivated. These episodes lack the ring of authenticity that Wouk achieves in his descriptions of life at sea.

A second theme with which Wouk deals at considerable length, and one related to his use of Willie as symbol of America, is the relationship between the career military officer and the reservist. An offshoot of what

Edgar Acken calls the "eternal conflict of ethics and standards between the military man and the civilian,"[27] *The Caine Mutiny* is a "case history of the average civilian of a free country who finds himself in wartime serving in the armed forces, who is astounded and often repelled by the service way of doing things" (McClean, 195). Willie Keith serves as a "symbol of the citizen of a democratic society coming into contact for the first time with a singleminded service officer and all that officer stands for" (Acken, 6). He is one of those "hundreds of officers" selected from the group of "college boys, salesmen, schoolteachers, lawyers, clerks, writers, druggists, engineers, farmers, piano players" who answered their country's call (*CM*, 246).

The idea certainly did not originate with Wouk. In fact, the pattern is typical, as Albert Van Nostrand explains: "The normal war novel is the saga of a group of private citizens assembled for military training and gradually built into a fighting unit . . . When this group finally meets the enemy, the citizen/soldiers test themselves at terrible cost, and the whole erosive experience yields only a muted hope for the few survivors" (Van Nostrand, 183). In novels about the army, the focus is usually on a platoon. Wouk varies the pattern slightly, setting his story aboard a small ship, where the commander is close to those who must act out his orders and whose lives are in danger when the captain makes wrong decisions. Wouk's novel is even more unusual in that the group aboard the *Caine* sees little actual combat. The difficult adjustment to be made by reservists Maryk, Keefer, Keith, and the other new ensigns, is to the myriad of rules that govern the conduct of everyday business in the navy. The conflict is deeper than it may seem; for not only is this a novel about the adjustment of individuals to a particular system that seems foreign to them; it is also a case study in "the conflict of individual liberty with totalitarian authority in time of war" (Carpenter, 213).

For most of the novel, Wouk appears consistent with the mainstream of American novelists who write about warfare: he presents "a service-blasting, liberal intellectual novel"[28] that highlights the mindlessness of regulations and procedures, an "ironic scrutiny of the whole naval system as it is mocked, hated, but obeyed by the civilian officers who did not graduate from the Academy."[29] Yet in the end he "celebrate[s] and uphold[s] the competence of the elites directing the forces' administrative hierarchy."[30] If one sees this as a simple dichotomy, it is easy to miss the point of Wouk's analysis of this peculiar American phenomenon. Spencer Brown believes that "Wouk undermines that reading with more complex and profound possibilities" (Brown, 599).

Wouk carefully introduces a number of career officers, all graduates of the Naval Academy, and a large contingent of reservists from all walks of life, who find themselves in positions of great responsibility as the war progresses. When Willie reports for duty aboard the *Caine*, the wardroom includes three U.S. Naval Academy graduates: DeVriess, Gorton (the executive officer), and Carmody. All prove to be competent sailors and leaders. Throughout the novel, Wouk introduces other "regulars," who are efficient without seeming to be martinets. Captain Grace of the service forces' headquarters offers Queeg sound advice about admitting mistakes and living up to his responsibilities as a commander (*CM*, 178–82). Captain White assumes command of the *Caine* after the mutiny, and turns the ship's morale around within five months (*CM*, 486).

These regulars are conscious of the presence of reservists, and often treat them with suspicion or even disdain. DeVriess warns Queeg that within a few months after the latter assumes command, the wardroom of the *Caine*—the entire contingent of officers serving under Queeg—is likely to be reserve officers (*CM*, 130). When the navy's chief legal officer in San Diego is considering which lawyers to appoint as Maryk's defense counsel, he hesitates to select Barney Greenwald because Greenwald is a reservist, and he fears the public will see the court-martial as a contest between regulars and reservists (*CM*, 378).

The reservists feel the stigma from their first days on active duty, and their second-class status haunts them throughout the war. So many reservists have problems in adjusting to "the navy way"—the system of rules and regulations that seem to make no sense. Willie learns while in midshipmen school that success in the navy requires memorizing the manuals, rather than understanding the jargon (*CM*, 28). Tom Keefer, who prides himself in having learned to manipulate the system to his advantage, is especially pleased at being able to dash off memos in bureaucratic prose using 10 words when one will do, and often saying nothing at all (*CM*, 176–77). For Keefer, the work in the navy is intentionally fragmented so that "a few excellent brains at the top" can manage the hundreds of thousands of "near-morons" who perform repetitive and seemingly mindless tasks (*CM*, 105). He believes the navy should be manned by men like Queeg, not people who can be useful in civilian society (*CM*, 218). Nevertheless, Keefer is fearful that the fraternity of regulars—he compares them at one point to the British ruling class (*CM*, 219)—is so protective of their own group that no reservist stands a chance in head-to-head conflict with someone like Queeg. Hence, when Maryk wants Keefer to accompany him to Admiral Halsey to bring Queeg's disabilities to the admiral's attention, Keefer warns him that the admiral will simply consider them "a couple of goddamn mutinous reserves" (*CM*, 342).

Critics have accused Wouk of needlessly siding with the regulars against the citizen/sailors who joined the navy in its moment of crisis. Barney Greenwald's speech to Maryk and Keefer after the court-martial, in which he seems to exonerate Queeg and condemn the mutineers for not supporting their incompetent captain, is most often cited in support of that judgment. Other evidence in the novel, however, suggests that Wouk sees a role for both regulars and reservists. While it is true that the regulars provide the necessary expertise to operate effectively under the extreme stress produced by war, no global conflict can be won by these professionals alone. Ensign Acres explains to Willie, when the latter visits him aboard a supply ship to which he has been assigned after a stint as an instructor at midshipmen school, everyone serving—even those who seemed to have easier tasks than the combat troops—are doing a necessary job, and most are doing it well (*CM*, 276). Willie reaches the same conclusion as he takes the *Caine* to the scrapheap. Reflecting on his experience, he realizes that, though his ship had not really accumulated a distinguished record in combat, the men of the *Caine* were doing what had to be done to preserve America—not necessarily to make it better, but simply to keep it alive as "the same old country we love" (*CM*, 527).

A final theme—and one that leads directly to the novel's mixed reception as a work of serious literature—is Wouk's analysis of the problems of command at sea. In this "penetrating study of the problems of command" (McClean, 195), Wouk manages to examine "the effects of command on an individual, the strains to which he is subjected, the breaking under pressure" (Browne, 217). Though the last phrase applies most directly to Queeg, I believe it describes Keefer as well, and that Wouk offers a more panoramic view of the problem than critics have generally acknowledged.

While it may be true that "the major portion of the book is devoted to the . . . character development of Lieutenant Commander Philip Francis Queeg" (Haley, 71), Wouk is careful to present numerous other commanders with whom the reader may compare him. Five men command the *Caine* before Willie becomes her last skipper: DeVriess, Queeg, Maryk, White, and Keefer. Each has distinguishing qualities which signal the attributes of a competent captain. Various other commanders are introduced for comparison, most notably Iron Duke

Sammis on one of the *Caine*'s sister ships; Willie learns early that the
spit-and-polish he sees aboard Sammis's ship belies his draconian treatment of subordinates.[31] Similarly, only after DeVriess leaves do Willie—
and the reader—learn that outward appearances belie the real measure
of a man's ability to command a naval vessel. This may be a rather obvious point, but it is still worth making. Sorting out the traits that distinguish a real commander from pretenders is something Willie and the
reader learn to do as the story progresses.

Of course, a central issue that interests Wouk is the role and responsibility of the ship's captain. "[T]he problem of command" in the novel,
B. R. McElderry says, "is formulated as a test case: granted that the theory of command is sound when a good officer is involved, does it hold
when the officer is incompetent to the point of endangering the lives of
his crew?"[32] Queeg not only lacks common sense; he is, as Robert
Bierstedt says, on more than one occasion "dangerous . . . He fails to do
what a reasonably prudent and capable seaman would do," believing
that following orders is more important than exercising even the small-
est amount of initiative (Bierstedt, 3). Numerous critics have also
observed that Queeg is a coward, a vindictive man who blames others
for his mistakes and who "uses privilege to his own advantage"
(Metraux, 41). James R. Browne believes it is "absurd" to claim that
Queeg buckles under the pressure of command, "when nowhere in the
book is he first shown as exercising command in even the most elementary competent way" (Browne, 217).

By the time of the mutiny, it is apparent to Maryk at least that the
ship is "being maneuvered in the storm by a captain who has already
proved himself a petty tyrant, an incipient paranoiac, and an incompetent in time of crisis" (Rogow, 17). The question about the proper course
of action for subordinates facing such a crisis is one of initiative. What
should be done? Maryk, who acts with "vigor and decision" (Bierstedt,
5), seems justified by preceding events to relieve the captain; the ship
and crew are in imminent danger.

That observation seems fair. Furthermore, Wouk spends considerable
time developing scenes in which the question of command takes center
stage, so that readers can form their own opinions about the qualities of
a good commander. For example, though he considers his first skipper a
tyrant, Willie recognizes that there is something about DeVriess's bearing—a quality not in his carriage or (slovenly) physical appearance—but
something in his manner, the look in his eye, his decisiveness in dealing

with issues great and small, that marks him as one capable of command (*CM*, 100). Though he will allow the physical appearance of the ship to deteriorate, DeVriess will not tolerate poor performance in operational drills. The crew seems to respond positively to such treatment, doing anything necessary to meet their captain's demands for excellence. Queeg, on the other hand, quickly establishes himself as a martinet, a self-proclaimed "book man" who nevertheless is willing to bend the rules when necessary for keeping his own record clean or benefitting personally from the privileges of command. His erratic behavior under pressure stems from his inability to handle the routine duties associated with ship command: the incident of his running aground and ripping the forecastle of another ship while maneuvering the *Caine* out of the harbor in Hawaii, almost his first official act as captain, clearly illustrates his incompetence (*CM*, 154). While he rants and raves at the crew about spit-and-polish issues, their safety often seems in jeopardy. Ensign Harding offers an assessment that may summarize Wouk's view. The function of the captain, he says, is "to get us out of jams," not simply to "check off due dates" on various assignments and reports (*CM*, 260).

Though he never consciously believes that Queeg may be suffering from some form of psychological disorder, Willie comes to the sad conclusion that his captain is well-meaning but unable to handle a job "beyond his powers" (*CM*, 327). Queeg simply does not have the capability to handle the position. Of course, this is to suggest that the navy made a mistake in assigning him as captain of the *Caine*. Viewed in this light, Queeg is simply the victim of the Peter Principle. Having risen above his level of competence, he now demonstrates the problem inherent in any hierarchy, where promotion and assumption of greater responsibility depend simply on demonstrating competence in assignments demanding lesser skills and talents. It may be true that, as the commander of the destroyer group testifies at the court-martial, the captain is trusted above all others to make right judgments because he has greater knowledge of the sea than anyone else aboard ship (*CM*, 440). Nevertheless, as events at the court-martial prove, command at sea presents the "greatest strain that can be brought to bear on a person" (*CM*, 476). Being in command, Keefer tells Willie near the end of the book, is "the loneliest, most oppressive job" he can imagine, a "nightmare" that forces one to walk a thin line between terrible alternatives if wrong decisions and errors in judgment are made (*CM*, 499).[33] Reflecting on the immense responsibility imposed on commanders, Willie writes to May that when one is forced to serve with a commander such as Queeg, the best course of action might be to do one's best to serve loyally (CM, 505).

Throughout the novel, Wouk rather insistently poses the question of what happens when the captain cannot measure up to the task of command. As I have suggested, his answer is rather enigmatic, and has been the source of much of the negative criticism the book has received. If Barney Greenwald's indictment of the mutiny can be taken at face value, Wouk seems to come down on the side of those who argue for blind obedience to command. Few Americans—especially American literary critics—can swallow such conservative medicine without gagging.

Critical Reception

Criticism of *The Caine Mutiny* is reminiscent of much that is written about Wouk's works. A few reviewers found much to praise in the novel. A larger group had more negative comments. These quickly divided into two camps: those who offered palliatives to explain the uneasy feeling they had in plodding along from one adventure to another, and those who confronted Wouk head-on for what they perceived as his unwillingness to accept the moral and social consequences of the action as he himself had written it.

A number of critics have given the novel high marks. Joseph Waldmeir, author of a critical study of the American war novel, believes that "Both Wouk and [James Gould] Cozzens write extremely well" and that *The Caine Mutiny* and *Guard of Honor* are "two of the best-made novels to come out of" World War II (Waldmeir, 136). While acknowledging the problems best-selling authors have with highbrow critics, Robert Bierstedt praised the novel for its "considerable literary merit" (Bierstedt, 1). The reviewer for the *Library Journal* succinctly recommended the novel: "Superb writing and deft characterization make this the most exciting sea story since *Mutiny on the Bounty*."[34] Another favorable review spoke of the novel as "provocative," "full of authentic people and atmosphere" (Acken, 6). The reviewer for *Catholic World* found that Wouk's novel "attempts something few war novels of any stature have tried: entertainment."[35]

The mildest critiques came from reviewers who found the book "a bit too long, at times too pat and literary"[36]; at least one warned readers that, "as usual in a story of men at war there are rough language and sex talk"[37]—this, about a novel in which the author prides himself in having left the "general obscenity and blasphemy of shipboard talk" "almost wholly unrecorded" because "its appearance in print annoys some readers" (*CM*, v).

More serious objections have always come from so-called highbrow critics, those associated with periodicals such as the *Atlantic, New Yorker, New York Times*, and those with academic affiliations. The demands of such critics often run counter to popular tastes; hence it is not unusual for Wouk's work, including *The Caine Mutiny*, to receive less favorable treatment from this group. In the case of *The Caine Mutiny*, F. I. Carpenter suggests that the novel's "simplicity and directness, attractive to the popular reader, has tended to repel the more sophisticated critic." Further, Carpenter notes, "much of the excellence" of the work "lies in the vivid reality of characters created without recourse to the psychological techniques of modernism" (Carpenter, 213).

For every critique like Carpenter's, however, there is at least one that calls into question the artistic and moral value of *The Caine Mutiny*. Some reviewers would simply dismiss the novel along with its author, claiming that the "comparative failure" of the novel is due simply to the fact that "Wouk is not a great writer." But, as the same reviewer notes, "certain paradoxes remain" (Brown, 599). James Browne postulates that "Although the rank of the book as a work of art does not directly concern us, we should be disposed to argue that a moral flaw in its structure, if such it be, is relevant to an esthetic judgement." He goes on to suggest that a "moral flaw" does indeed lurk at the center of Wouk's story: a flaw involving Wouk's ultimate judgement about his captain and the mutineers. The work has turned out to be "provocative," "not because it is a profound book, inducing deep reflections or arousing controversies or important intellectual or public issues," but rather because of the "puzzling distinction introduced by the author toward the end of the story" (Browne, 216). At the end of the novel, Wouk "springs a wholly unprepared-for surprise," absolving Queeg and placing the blame for the captain's problems on his "ambitious and cowardly subordinates" (Stuckey, 159). In a damning commentary, Harvey Swados sees the problem as twofold: a willful deception on the part of the author, and a willing reception of the lie by an American reading public ready for the pablum Wouk offers. Wouk, he says, wants to "let us have our cake and eat it, to stimulate us, without unduly provoking us, to make us feel that we are thinking without really forcing us to think . . . What the new middle class wanted—and found in *The Caine Mutiny*—was an assurance that its years of discomfort and hardship in the Second World War were not in vain, and that its sacrifices in a permanent war economy, and its gradual accommodation to the emergence of the military as a dominant element in civil life have been not only necessary, but praiseworthy" (Swados, 255). What B. R. McElderry calls the "reversal" at the end of the novel is a "conspicuous failure," since "nearly 90 percent of the book tears Queeg down. Only the last 50 pages attempt to build him up, and then only through the abstract principle of command, not by the visible actions of Queeg himself" (McElderry, 131).

Such harsh charges deserve careful attention. Perhaps the best way to judge their merit, and hence to determine if the novel is actually so seriously flawed as to deny it a place among the best American novels, is to review the specific scene that has provoked these attacks—Barney Greenwald's amazing denunciation of the mutineers (and especially Tom Keefer) after he has managed to get Maryk acquitted of all charges. The scene has been called "maudlin" (Bierstedt, 9), an unnecessary attack on the men who acted in good faith to save their ship and crew from an "incompetent madman."[38] To fully understand Wouk's motives requires a careful review of his portrayal of Queeg and Keefer, the two characters whose conduct up to that point leads readers to conclude that mutiny is justified. Many reviewers see this conclusion as denied by Greenwald's attack at the "victory" celebration after the court-martial.

Philip Francis Queeg reports to the *Caine* as its commander having served in the navy for 14 years, eight at sea, four aboard a carrier. He makes it clear at the outset of his tour as captain that he is a "book man" and that he expects his people to follow regulations meticulously (*CM*, 140). However, in his first act as captain he handles the ship poorly, gashing a hole in another ship and grounding the *Caine* in the mud (*CM*, 154–55). This incompetence might be attributed to nervousness or unfamiliarity with the new ship; but Queeg compounds the problem by trying to cover up the incident, and then by blaming others for misunderstanding his commands (*CM*, 156). He panics when he has to direct his ship out of port in a fog (*CM*, 164–67), then flies into a rage when he sees a sailor working with his shirttail out (*CM*, 168–69). In almost every instance, an officer or a member of the crew observes Queeg's behavior.

Added to his incompetence and his haste to blame others is his inability to make a decision. After the *Caine* loses a target (a rather expensive piece of equipment), Queeg cannot decide if the ship should retrieve it and return late to port, or sail back to the harbor and let someone else find the gear. For this he is rebuked by one of his superiors, who believes he is unintelligent and rather undistinguished among his Naval Academy classmates (*CM*, 180–82).

These early incidents would be mere annoyances, but Queeg continues to perform in ways that alienate his subordinates and endanger the lives of his crew and others. The novel's fourth and fifth sections are a catalog of the captain's errors and petty reprisals. As the men grow to hate him, Queeg increasingly isolates himself. At Maryk's court-martial, Queeg distorts events to present himself in a favorable light, failing to recall some events that have been clearly described in the narrative, prevaricating about other issues, and insinuating that some members of his crew are homosexuals or cowards (*CM*, 462–69).

Ironically, only Steve Maryk stands by the captain, reprimanding junior officers who speak against him. Maryk acts as a loyal subordinate, even though he recognizes that the ship has inherited a skipper far inferior to DeVriess. He is not blind to Queeg's deficiencies, but he is willing to work with the captain to accomplish the ship's missions. Only when Keefer points out that Queeg may be suffering from some form of mental disorder does the executive officer begin to look for a pattern in Queeg's behavior. In a very real sense, Keefer plants the seeds of mutiny in Maryk's mind; there is, then, some justice to Greenwald's accusation that Keefer is the real "author" of the mutiny. When the captain appears unable to respond logically at the height of the typhoon, Maryk is already predisposed to mutiny. Wouk is vague about the rightness or wrongness of Maryk's decision to face the ship into the wind. As several people testify at the court-martial, only the captain on the scene can determine the right course of action under such circumstances. By taking command, Maryk shifts responsibility for that crucial decision from Queeg to himself; whether Queeg would have ever made the right decision remains eternally open to question.

Willie sees Queeg a bit differently, however. On numerous occasions, Willie sees his captain consciously avoiding enemy fire as he maneuvers the ship in combat operations (*CM*, 295). Bluntly, this is personal cowardice, an inexcusable quality in a person selected to command. Much hinges on the reader's understanding of the significance of Willie's observations. Incompetence can be compensated; blame improperly laid on the wrong people can be shifted to those actually responsible. Cowardice, on the other hand, simply cannot be tolerated. Of course, if Willie's observations are inaccurate, then Queeg is not really guilty of a flaw that would demand relief from command.

Wouk remains intentionally vague about Queeg's behavior, using point-of-view to great advantage in masking his own attitudes about his fictional captain. Readers see the story from various angles; we are allowed into the minds of a number of characters, but Queeg's thoughts are kept from us. Hence, the captain's motives are constantly, if subtly, in question. Our question about Queeg is similar to the one we have asked about Hamlet for almost 400 years: is he mad, or simply clever? We simply do not know if Queeg is psychologically unfit for command, or if the job is simply too big for him. If the latter is true, then a loyal wardroom could indeed have covered for him in times of stress, building a relationship of trust that would have allowed him to be more open with them and more reliant on their abilities to make up for his deficiencies. If, however, Queeg is paranoid (or otherwise mentally imbalanced), no amount of effort on the part of Maryk and the other officers would compensate for this deficiency.

We simply have no good way of knowing which interpretation is correct. Clearly Greenwald thinks the captain could have been saved, had the members of his wardroom displayed some loyalty. Most critics hold that Greenwald is speaking for Wouk himself when he exonerates the captain. Albert Van Nostrand calls Greenwald "Wouk's spokesman," and goes on to excoriate the author for "indict[ing] the mutineers on the grounds that they are accountable for their irresponsibility—a condition for which he pardons Queeg at the same time. Either his pardon or his indictment is illogical." What Wouk is trying to do, Van Nostrand says, is to "shuffle" his attitudes "so that nearly everybody wins" (Van Nostrand, 199). Certainly that is Allen Guttmann's view, who criticizes Wouk for what he believes is a conscious shift of focus at the end of the book. "Incident after incident demonstrates Queeg's absolute unfitness to command a ship," he notes, but Greenwald's speech "reverses" the "emotional vectors" by asserting that Queeg was right all the time. Wouk's position, Guttmann argues, is that "the military establishment that fought and defeated Nazi Germany must be affirmed by grateful Jews" (Guttmann, 21).

Wouk's handling of the captain's behavior—deemed a flaw by readers who reject Wouk's ambiguity, and a strength for those who see it as essential to a complex portrait of command—leaves the reader to judge for himself whether Queeg is insane or incompetent, and if the other officers could have made up for his deficiencies. The portrayal of the villain, Lieutenant Tom Keefer, is less vague. More than any other man, Keefer remains wholly unredeemed as a malcontent who willfully ignores the demands of the service, shirking his duty whenever he can and castigating the system that he finds fit only for idiots, morons, and men of ox-like sensibilities. Typically, Keefer is the modern intellectual— a frequent target of Wouk's criticism, who comes under special fire in *The Caine Mutiny*.

Even before Tom Keefer appears in the story, readers know something about him, because Tom's brother, Roland, is one of Willie's roommates at midshipman's school. When Roland learns of Willie's assignment to the *Caine*, he mentions that his brother is aboard the ship, and warns Willie not to take anything his brother says about the ship or the navy too seriously. Tom, he says, is a "three-dollar bill"; the ship is probably fine if Tom has nothing good to say about it (*CM*, 69). When they first meet in Keefer's quarters aboard the *Caine*, Willie notices that his personal library contains works by T. S. Eliot, Joyce, Proust, Dos Passos, Kafka, Freud, and books on psychoanalysis (*CM*, 78). Later in the novel, when Keefer has the chance to speak to a group of college coeds, he quotes liberally from these same writers, as well as from Gertrude Stein, Hart Crane, Thomas Mann, and Thomas Wolfe (*CM*, 220). Wouk finds most of these writers "offensive" (Stuckey, 161).[39]

Keefer, officially the communications officer, spends all of his free time (and much of his time that should be devoted to official matters) working on a novel, or reading Joyce's *Finnegan's Wake* (*CM*, 244). He resents the fact that, while at the same age men like Dickens, George Meredith, and Richard Brinsley Sheridan were writing masterpieces, he has been forced to spend his time decoding navy messages (*CM*, 99). In a revealing moment, he admits to Willie that he resents Queeg primarily because the new skipper has "slowed the progress of American litera-ture" by preventing him from making significant progress on his book (*CM*, 306).

At first, Willie defends Keefer, claiming that if Keefer produces a fine novel from his navy experiences he will make a "greater contribution to America" than those handling military tasks. Ensign Carmody—a Naval Academy graduate—replies sagely, "His assignment is communications, not contributions to America" (*CM*, 103). A perennial critic of the navy way, Keefer brags of his ability to master the system—he tells Willie that dashing off memoranda in navy prose is actually enjoyable, because he can be "like a concert pianist improvising on chopsticks" (*CM*, 177). Eventually, however, Willie learns that the complicated "navy" system Keefer has shown him for keeping track of message traffic was actually invented by Keefer and former communications officers; the navy way, which the ship's yeoman shows him, is much simpler (*CM*, 244–45). At this point, Keefer's weaknesses are becoming apparent both to Willie, and to the reader.

Unfortunately, Steve Maryk is unable to divine the novelist's ulterior motives for wanting to remove Queeg from command. Greenwald is certainly correct in his denunciation of Keefer as the real brain behind the mutiny. Keefer first suggests to Maryk that the captain has psychological problems (*CM*, 285), though he is unwilling to make such observations known to a competent medical authority for fear that he will be accused of conspiring to "undermine authority" (*CM*, 290). Not only does he continue to prod Maryk to see paranoia in everything Queeg does; he even points out to the executive officer the relevant articles in naval regulations under which a commander may be relieved (*CM*, 324). When he reads Maryk's log of the captain's behavior, he tells him it is "a clinical picture of a paranoiac, a full case history" (*CM*, 336); yet, when they visit Admiral Halsey to report their observations, Keefer finds a host of excuses for refusing to confront the fleet commander, pointing out that much of what Queeg had done could be explained logically (*CM*, 339). Small wonder that there is confusion about Queeg's sanity; the chief perpetrator of the idea of the captain's mental imbalance cannot bring himself to jeopardize his future by making this discovery public. Instead, as Greenwald points out, Keefer manages to get others to take all the risks in toppling Queeg, carefully keeping his own "skirts all white and starchy" (*CM*, 483).

No matter how one judges Queeg, it is impossible not to blame Keefer for much of what has happened aboard the *Caine*. He represents what Wouk considers the worst in America's civilian population: he is a lazy intellectual, unwilling to roll up his sleeves and get to work to save the country that has given him the opportunity to succeed in his chosen profession. Worse, he achieves his success at the expense of the system that protects him. There is not an ounce of redeeming grace in Keefer's attitude toward the navy, and by extension, to other American institutions. Not surprisingly, when he is thrust into command, Keefer is unable to perform better than the men he criticized; the wine Barney Greenwald tosses on him at the victory party becomes his Yellow Stain, marking him (like the biblical Cain) as a coward. As the *Caine*'s commander, he behaves much like Queeg, isolating himself from his men and handling the ship poorly (*CM*, 487). Whereas Queeg's cowardice is only insinuated, Keefer's is plainly seen. When the *Caine* is in danger after being hit by a kamikaze pilot, he abandons the ship—clutching the manuscript of his novel (*CM*, 489).

It may be true, as B. R. McElderry observes, that "Keefer is too convenient to be convincing" (McElderry, 132). Whether Keefer's "perfidy" is "the perfidy of a class" (Bierstedt, 14) may be questioned by some critics, but the author's answer is clear. This man, Wouk says through his text, is no hero. He is no one to emulate. He is wrong about America, about the navy, about life. If America is smart, Wouk implies, it will reject him as a role model just as Willie Keith has rejected him.

Whether Queeg is to be seen as a hero or a goat, the preponderance of evidence suggests that his relief was correct under the circumstances. Greenwald's argument at the victory party on Queeg's behalf is really no different than his brilliant performance in defending Maryk and destroying the credibility of the captain; both can be seen as exercises in courtroom theatrics, intentionally muddying the waters, and upsetting the confidence of the smug officers who are so sure that, because they did the right thing in one circumstance, their assessment of the navy as an organization unfit for America's best and brightest is correct. Greenwald's denunciation is meant less to exonerate Queeg personally, but rather to remind these reservists that men like him are a vital part of American society, deserving of our admiration and respect.

Such strident conservative views have given many critics reason to argue with Wouk. Frankly, many people, especially literary scholars, are uncomfortable confronting such stridency in a work that has achieved a degree of popularity denied to many more liberal works. Joseph Waldmeir hits the mark with his assessment of the novelist's attitude: Wouk, like James Gould Cozzens, is unabashedly conservative in presenting his view of warfare, to the point of defending, on occasion, "fascist tendencies in America or in her armed forces" as "expediencies" in times of war, and attacking those "who protest them" (Waldmeir, 125). Wouk's philosophical position is clear, and *The Caine Mutiny* is designed to deliver it to the American reading public.

The Caine Mutiny on Stage and Screen

Flushed with his novel's success, Wouk decided that before beginning a new work of fiction, he would capitalize on the fame of *The Caine Mutiny* and satisfy his lifelong love of theater by turning his story into a play. During 1952 and 1953 he worked to convert the "blockbuster" novel (over 400 pages in any edition) into a drama that could be staged in an evening. The pared-down version runs to a mere 100 pages of dialogue and stage directions, but like its fictional cousin, *The Caine Mutiny Court-Martial* enjoyed immediate success and has continued to play to packed audiences in both amateur and professional performances.

The technical problem of reducing such a massive novel into a manageable script seems daunting. Wouk solved this dilemma by focusing on the most "dramatic" element of his novel, Maryk's court-martial. Though that event takes up just slightly more than 100 pages of the novel, and serves as the culmination of 300 pages of events, Wouk manages to insert sufficient background information about his characters and the conflicts that led up to Maryk's relief of Queeg in lengthy sections of dialogue in the first act. Though *New York Times* critic Brooks Atkinson commented in his first review of the play that this part of the drama tends to be a bit talky and that it drags somewhat when staged,[40] he was impressed enough to remark in a second column about the production that "Since 420 pages of narrative [in the first edition] precede the trial scene in the novel, Mr. Wouk's talent for compression is virtually superhuman, and should be the envy of newspaper copyeditors." He goes on to call *The Caine Mutiny Court-Martial* "one of the two or three most dramatic plays of the season."[41]

From these early conversations, playgoers gleen the necessary information to understand the nature of Queeg's tenure as commander. In act two, Wouk strips away the descriptions that flesh out the courtroom drama in section six of his novel, leaving virtually intact the exchanges between Barney Greenwald and the witnesses who parade before the board of officers.

Some inkling of the play's success was evident even before it opened in New York. The pre-Broadway run, begun in the fall of 1953 in California, where many navy sympathizers were sure to be in the audience, received favorable notices nationwide.[42] The cast of the Broadway production that opened on 20 January 1954, included Lloyd Nolan as Queeg and Henry Fonda as Barney Greenwald. Directed by Charles Laughton and produced by Paul Gregory, *The Caine Mutiny Court-Martial* enjoyed an immensely successful run—415 performances—and won Wouk a place in Broadway history. It enjoyed similar success in London in 1956—as Wouk noted he attended the premier of the play at the Hippodrome on June 13 and "heard a huge London audience acclaim" the work.[43] There can be little doubt that, for the gagman who had wanted for so long to succeed as a playwright, and who had hitherto achieved only modest success in his first medium of choice, the accolades he received for this drama were especially pleasing.

The reasons for the play's success are numerous. One critic wryly observed that "nothing could look less theatrical" than this "intensely dramatic" production; because Wouk "dispenses with heroics" and "avoids purple patches" in order to "concentrate on the subject at hand," he makes an earnest attempt to grapple with a serious moral issue.[44] More interesting for literary scholars is the fact that, in transforming his novel into a play, Wouk essentially changed the focus of events and—perhaps even more importantly—changed his hero. *The Caine Mutiny* is Willie Keith's story; the trials at sea, the conflicts between the commander and his men, are all part of a larger work that shows the reader Willie's maturation. In *The Caine Mutiny Court-Martial,* Barney Greenwald assumes center stage, as Wouk focuses on questions of authority and responsibility, on the conflict between the military bureaucracy represented by Queeg (symbol of the "regulars") and the civilian soldier (represented by both Maryk and Greenwald). Willie Keith's is little more than a walk-on role.[45]

The Hollywood movie version of *The Caine Mutiny* is another matter. Though he had previously dabbled in the movies, Wouk was not an accomplished screenwriter, so the task of reducing his book to a movie script fell to veteran screenwriter Stanley Roberts.[46] As one might expect, some of the novel simply could not fit into the confines of the film medium. The movie opens, for example, with Willie Keith's graduation from officer candidate school, omitting his early troubles recounted in the novel's first 50 pages. Even this pared-down script drew criticism from a number of reviewers. One observed that, "in preparing the complicated script," screenwriter Roberts "endeavored to cram into the picture more of the novel than was required." The love interest that runs throughout the book becomes "useless and artless" in the screen version.[47] Another critic, writing some years after the movie was released, suggested that this "slow, somewhat unimaginative film" is partially redeemed, however, "by Humphrey Bogart's superb performance as the tragic, demoralized Captain Queeg.[48]

Unquestionably, the commercial success of the movie can be attributed in large part to the casting. Van Johnson, accomplished at playing all-American figures, exudes sincerity and competence as Steve Maryk. Fred MacMurray portrays the hypocritical Tom Keefer with sufficient unctuousness to bring him alive as a sophisticated villain. José Ferrer's Barney Greenwald (a curious bit of casting) comes across as strong-

willed and angry, making his climactic denunciation of Keefer and the
mutineers compelling and credible.[49] And of course, the crowning
achievement of the picture is Humphrey Bogart's portrayal of Captain
Queeg. The "film's action centers on Queeg's deterioration," and
Bogart's rendition of the captain leaves little doubt that Queeg is suffering from some kind of psychopathic condition.[50] Bogart, already a
Hollywood legend when *The Caine Mutiny* was released, gave an aston-
ishing rendition of Wouk's pathetic captain; his nervous, twitchy, stut-
tering Queeg has become ingrained in the minds of generations of
Americans who have seen the film. There is, however, a certain irony in
this phenomenon. In the novel, Wouk describes Queeg as slightly bald-
ing, a bit paunchy, and rather stern and overbearing. There is no sugges-
tion that he is a walking bag of nervous tics; of course, the captain does
roll his little steel balls when confronted with a crisis (and many things
are a crisis to Queeg). Nevertheless, Wouk's captain is a youngish 36;
Bogart is clearly an aging commander, whose haggard appearance gives
the impression that he is near total exhaustion and physical breakdown.
Yet when, in a mid-1980s television movie of the court-martial, Queeg
was played by an actor who looked much more like the captain
described in the novel, many people were disappointed; they felt the
captain was "too young," that he "didn't look at all like the seasoned
veteran whom the navy would be assigning to command a combat vessel," that he was "gruff, rather than paranoid."[51] One can only wonder
what Wouk thought of the new television version; it seems clear,
though, that this production is in many ways closer to the spirit of the
novel than the 1954 Hollywood movie.

  Whatever Hollywood did to transform this novel into a movie, at the
time the changes seemed right. Although a number of critics found the
pace of the movie slow and the action decidedly undramatic (Crowther,
17), the American Academy of Motion Pictures lauded the effort and
rewarded it with several Academy Award nominations. The film was
nominated for Best Picture. Bogart was nominated as Best Actor, and
Tom Tully, who played DeVriess, as Best Supporting Actor. Stanley
Roberts received a nomination for the screenplay, John Livadary for
sound direction, Max Steiner for the score, William A. Lyon and Henry
Batista for the editing. By the end of the 1960s, the film had ascended
to the level of "classic"; along with the play and the novel, it has continued to afford the American public a portrait of the citizen/sailor and to
celebrate the role of the many unnamed and unsung heroes of America's
greatest twentieth-century conflict.

Concurrently, the story of Queeg, Maryk, Keith, and Keefer secured Herman Wouk a place in American popular cultural history. However one judges the novel's ultimate literary merit, Wouk considered his popular success more important than pleasing the highbrow literary community. For like his literary idol, Dickens, he has contributed to the folklore of his country by creating a figure who lives beyond the confines of his novel. Scores of people who have never read *The Caine Mutiny* or seen the movie or play nevertheless have heard of Captain Queeg, and are familiar with those little steel balls rolling nervously in the palm of the captain's hand.

Chapter Four

Writing for the Masses

Growing up Jewish: *Marjorie Morningstar*

According to William S. Hudson, at an early stage in his career as a novelist Herman Wouk had decided that, once he had become confident in his abilities as a storyteller, he would "write two novels as an attempt to master the novel-writing craft. In the first of these he would experiment with narration; in the second, he would concentrate on characterization. The results of this lengthy experiment were *The Caine Mutiny* and *Marjorie Morningstar*."[1] The first was an international best-seller, still read and subjected to critical scrutiny; the history of the second, however, has been a bit more enigmatic. For in *Marjorie Morningstar*, Wouk returned to a subject he knew intimately—the Jewish-American community in which he had been raised—and this intimacy is the source of both its strengths and weaknesses.

The genesis of the novel is a play that Wouk wrote in 1940, a slight comedic piece he titled *Crisis over Marjorie*. In that work, the central action concerns the choice a young Jewish girl must make between two suitors—one a dashing but empty poseur, the other a more stolid, traditional fellow who eventually wins this Marjorie's affections and her hand. Marjorie's doting parents, residents of Central Park West, seem unable to manage their headstrong daughter, but a wise grandmother negotiates events so that the villainous young suitor Noel is exposed as a liar, and Marjorie is led to see that the more traditional young man, Sam Schwartz, is actually a better choice for a husband.[2]

Many of the characters from this 1940 drama find their way almost unchanged into the novel Wouk began sometime after 1950. A summary of the plot can help make clear Wouk's major aims for the work. Marjorie Morgenstern, seventeen, is the daughter of Jewish immigrants who have managed to build a small nest egg through hard work in the import business. Their modest success has allowed them to move from the Bronx to Central Park West in New York City. The Morgensterns' dream is to give their children a better life than they had; for Marjorie, that means marrying her off to a respectable (and preferably well-to-do) Jewish boy who will provide for the girl and give them grandchildren.

Not surprisingly, Marjorie has other ideas. Attractive and highly self-confident, she has no trouble attracting young men's attention. In the novel's opening chapters, she tosses aside her first love, a rather ordinary young man from the Bronx, in favor of pursuing more appropriate catches in Manhattan. Her enrollment in Hunter College gives her the opportunity she needs to play the field, and though she is always slightly ashamed of having to attend the "subway college," as she disparagingly considers it, she achieves some notoriety among her co-ed classmates, especially after she takes up acting. At Hunter her dream of becoming Marjorie Morningstar is born; she vows then that she will not be just another Jewish housewife, but instead will make her mark on Broadway.

Marjorie is encouraged to pursue her aspirations by Marsha Zelenko, a Hunter College classmate who has her own dreams of achieving fame as a designer. Working together in theater, the two plot a future of stardom for Marjorie and financial success for Marsha. Through Marsha, Marjorie lands a summer job at Camp Tamarack, a refuge for youngsters from New York. The Morgensterns, who never warm to Marsha, are not pleased at the prospect of their daughter spending her summer just across the lake from South Wind, an adult camp that Mrs. Morgenstern describes as Sodom. Of course, the highlight of Marjorie's summer is a clandestine night visit to South Wind, where she meets the camp's social director, Noel Airman.

The remainder of Wouk's novel is centered largely on Marjorie's lengthy romance with Noel. Though her first visit to South Wind convinces Marjorie that she is in love with this bohemian composer and playwright, Noel pays only slight attention to the teenage interloper. Not until the following summer, when (against her parents' wishes) she lands a job at South Wind is she able to inject herself into Noel's life. Using her feminine wiles under the loose supervision of her beloved Uncle Samsom-Aaron, who has been given a job at South Wind through the influence of the Morgensterns, Marjorie eventually makes Noel fall for her. The difference in their ages—he is already 30, she not yet 21—makes most of the camp staff believe that this is simply another of Noel's many casual affairs. Marjorie knows better, however; though she says to everyone who asks that she is willing to continue her relationship with Noel on any terms, it is clear she is really interested in marriage. Despite her professed disdain for the customs and mores of her Jewish heritage, Marjorie is hesitant to indulge in an illicit sexual liaison. The moment of her greatest temptation comes after a day of gaiety when her parents, visiting the camp, seem to accept Noel as a possible husband for her. Marjorie is "saved" from having to succumb to the social director's amorous advances by the novel's one really tragic incident: her uncle, who had been featured in the festivities on this special day, is discovered floating in the camp's fountain, dead of a heart attack.

The death of Samson-Aaron at South Wind prompts Marjorie to return home, where for the next several years she pursues her twin goals: establishing herself as an actress, and getting Noel Airman to marry her. Though she has many auditions, no paying jobs come her way. Unscrupulous producers try to lure her into getting money from her parents to back their shows, but she seems unable to land a role on her talent alone. While her classmates from Hunter marry and become mothers, she remains the attractive but unattached starlet, approaching what for her is the catastrophic situation of being 25 and without any settled prospects for the future.

During these years, Marjories's relationship with Noel suffers a series of reversals. At one moment, the vagabond composer promises to take up a middle-class lifestyle so he can make himself more acceptable as a husband and son-in-law; he even accepts nine-to-five jobs on occasion, but quickly loses interest in such work and reverts to his more unconventional lifestyle. On a whim, he dashes off to Mexico, and later to Hollywood, as he works on various theatrical and movie projects. Meanwhile, Marjorie vacillates in her attachment to him, at times feeling that she must have him or die, at other moments giving him up and seeking the companionship of other men. Not until her friend Marsha is married—to a man well over 50—does Marjorie finally succumb to Noel's sexual advances and become his mistress.

But even the loss of her virginity does not guarantee that Noel Airman will marry her. Dejected at the failure of his first Broadway show, Airman leaves New York for Europe. Marjorie tries to put him out of her mind, but eventually she takes a job so that she can earn money and join him on the continent. With financial help from her parents, she books passage for Europe; aboard ship she meets Mike Eden, a zealous Jew working just on the edge of the law to help his kinsmen escape from prewar Nazi Germany. Eden finally makes Marjorie realize that Noel Airman is not as heroic as she imagines. When she tracks Noel down in Paris, they enjoy a bittersweet moment: he offers her a serious proposal of marriage, and she refuses.

In an epilogue, the reader learns that Marjorie Morningstar became what Noel Airman had always predicted she would be: Mrs. Milton Schwartz, a good Jewish mother, living in the suburbs, active in her temple and community. The would-be actress has exchanged her dreams of life in the limelight for the respectable alternative of carrying on the traditions of her people.

Wouk's sources for this involved story are manifold. In her master's thesis on the novel, Nancy Dawson found unconscious borrowings from Charlotte Brontë, Charles Dickens, Anthony Trollope, Lewis Carroll, and others.[3] Basic to the story is the author's own background, the New York of his boyhood and the Jewish home in which he grew up. His decision to write the story from the point of view of a young woman may seem a bit daring, but the idea had been germinating for more than a decade when he finally turned his attention to the work.[4] Perhaps because he knew the details of Marjorie's environment so well, he was able to generate a sense of realism that readers appreciated. Editor LeBaron Barker of Doubleday bought the book "on the basis of a 10-minute description before a line of it was written."[5] *Marjorie Morningstar* was a Book-of-the-Month Club selection in September 1955. Shortly after its publication, *Time* magazine did a cover story on the author. The rights were sold to Hollywood—and Wouk profited handsomely from the deal. The first printing, 100,000 copies, sold out in a week. The novel rocketed to the top of the best-seller list shortly after its publication in October 1955, and recorded the highest sales of any work of fiction that year. While it did not show the staying power of *The Caine Mutiny*, which topped the list for 21 months, commercially the novel did quite well. The high rate of sales and the heavy coverage of the work in popular magazines and newspapers assured it a place among the top performers in the commercial fiction market.[6]

A Novel of Customs and Maturation

Wouk's sprawling story of a young Jewish girl struggling to achieve her adolescent dreams, only to reject them in favor of a more traditional role, prompted the usual—and somewhat predictable—round of criticism. A sympathetic reviewer observed that the novel deals primarily with "the evolution of a young woman's personality and sense of values," and that the plot is woven "from three main strands: Marjorie's determination to be an actress; her protracted love affair with an attractive, talented but too volatile young man, and the strength of the Jewish family ideal."[7]

That succinct summary of the novel as a tale of maturation is correct—
as far as it goes. Wouk himself called *Marjorie Morningstar* a love story,
but few reviewers or critics have accepted his simple explanation. Most
have seen it as a heavily didactic work, an attempt on the part of the
author to once again affirm the value of conservatism and conformity.
"The book has powerful after-waves," one reviewer waxes, "[Wouk's]
theme would seem to be that the greater creativity is in conservation of
the central values of society."[8] R. T. Horchler calls the novel "less a
romance than a strenuously didactic moral and sociological study."[9]
Allen Guttmann goes so far as to attribute the novel's popularity to its
moral dimension: "It responded to a call that more talented writers
refused to answer. It provided a full, if somewhat inept, dramatization of
moral death and resurrection . . ."[10]

Robert Fitch offers an even more extensive explanation of Wouk's
intent. In one of the fullest critical examinations of the novel written to
date, Fitch observes: "There may be some readers who still think *Marjorie
Morningstar* is a love story. Of course it is nothing of the sort. It is an
account of the grim struggle for existence between two competing and
incompatible energies . . . the Bourgeois and the Bohemian."[11] Wouk
uses these terms in the novel, usually putting them in the mouth of Noel
Airman as he attempts to "educate" Marjorie about the ways of modern
society. For all her attempts to rebel against her parents and her heritage,
Marjorie is essentially bourgeois. Noel is Wouk's bohemian—though
Fitch believes the author has stacked the deck against the shiftless composer, making him a spineless ne'er-do-well, and a less compelling alternative than he might have been. Fitch goes on to elaborate how these
"two sides of an identical coin" operate within the novel: "Each of them
has an equal passion for success . . . Both . . . subscribe to the myth of
maturity. And naturally each claims for himself the sanction of the myth.
. . . [N]either the Bourgeois nor the Bohemian understands either sex or
love . . . Neither the Bourgeois nor the Bohemian is capable of a great
passion" (Fitch, 140–41). Both are hypocrites, Fitch explains, the bourgeois in the realm of ethics, the bohemian in the area of aesthetics. "The
Bohemian gets his biggest kick out of life when he titillates the compla-
cent Bourgeois; and the Bourgeois experiences the supreme thrill of
virtue when he contemplates the alluring sin which he lusts after but still
rejects" (Fitch, 142). For the reader who has made it to the end of Wouk's
750-page novel, Fitch's theory is certainly at least partially convincing.

To see the novel simply as a moral conflict between conservatism and
liberalism would be to miss much of Wouk's point. In what might be

termed a transformed autobiography, *Marjorie Morningstar* is an investigation of what it means—or at least what it meant for Wouk—to grow
up as an Orthodox Jew in America. The great threat to this essentially
conservative, traditionalist faith in a society like the United States is not
overt persecution, though some prejudice and discrimination continues
to exist. Rather, the evil antagonist against which Jews must struggle to
preserve their identity is the demon of assimilation. If *Marjorie
Morningstar* is, in a sense, a "handbook of middleclass Jewish life,"[12] it is
equally, as Mark Charney has noted, a story of "the conflicts inherent in
attempting to live by both Jewish and American standards," and of "the
struggle young American Jews experience in coming to terms with the
traditions of their elders."[13] Charney believes that, beneath the novel's
soap opera facade, Wouk has managed to "write in an honest, interesting manner of customs, traditions, and conflicts" Marjorie knows
(Charney, 385), and which she must ultimately affirm in order to take
her place in the society that has nurtured her in her adolescent years.
"What the story conveys," Maxwell Geismar remarks, "and quite often
brilliantly, is the tragicomic meeting of traditional Jewish culture and
the American success myth."[14]

If the novel is seen in this light, then Noel Airman is not simply a
free-thinking bohemian who tempts Marjorie to abandon conventional
ideas about sex. He is the lapsed Jew, an assimilationist who believes the
rituals of his family's religion are so much hokum. Insofar as she represents the traditional Jewish community, Marjorie is being pressed not
simply to abandon her moral code; she is asked to give up an entire way
of life. This is no soap opera plot, and Wouk takes the subject quite seriously. Though "Wouk's young heroes are rebels against the Jewish tradition, and the author gives every appearance of taking very seriously
indeed the arguments they present to justify their rebellion," it is clear
that the novelist is on the side of the tradition which Noel and Marjorie
(at least for a time) reject.[15] As Norman Podhoretz notes, Wouk "writes
out of a strong sense that Jewish life as such is severely constricted in its
possibilities, out of a feeling that the Jewish personality can only disinte-
grate and wither away if it ventures beyond the moral and spiritual confines of a Judaic bourgeois style." This in part "accounts for the sad tones
of the novel."[16]

The extensive description of Jewish life and customs is not simply a
backdrop for the heroine's love affair. There is specific purpose to the
descriptions of events such as the bar mitzvah of Marjorie's brother Seth
and the seder that degenerates into a series of hilarious mishaps as the

five-year-old son of Marjorie's cousin plays havoc with the adults and children in attendance. Wouk wants his readers to see the importance of such rituals in the lives of these people. Marjorie's agony over breaking traditional Jewish dietary laws is not just a metaphor of rebellion. Wouk wants his readers to realize that the laws themselves play an important part in the lives of Orthodox Jews, helping to define their culture and their special relationship to their God. For this reason, Podhoretz is not quite accurate in criticizing Wouk for seeming to ignore Marjorie's feelings about these laws. "The fact that the dietary laws have little meaning in her life never occurs to Wouk as an explanation [for Marjorie's willingness to break them], because that would drive him to wonder whether there might not be something to question in the dietary laws themselves that would force him really to grapple with the issue" (Podhoretz, 186). In Wouk's view, mature individuals accept the tenets of religion without demanding personal explanations; only the immature seek immediate reasons for following the rules. Wouk had undergone a life crisis similar to Marjorie's, having abandoned his religious practices for almost a decade during the 1930s. Though it may not be apparent in the novel, the author is looking back at his own crisis of faith in describing Marjorie's struggles.

Similarly, though Wouk's depiction of the evils of South Wind may seem "too simplistic," this "archetypal Jewish adult summer camp"[17] is clearly intended to serve both the sociological and moral purposes of his novel. The summer camp may be a contemporary Sodom (as Mrs. Morgenstern describes it on more than one occasion), a symbol of the evils of modern life. Simultaneously, however, it represents an even more immediate threat to the Orthodox Jewish way of life: people at South Wind behave like other Americans, putting their Jewishness aside to appear like anyone else. Even in their better efforts, they resemble the generic American well-to-do more than the upper classes of the Jewish community. Such a circumstances saddens Wouk, and he wants readers to see that something wonderful has been lost in their attempts to pursue the American dream.

Marjorie Morningstar's Literary Qualities

Since *Marjorie Morningstar* has been called one of Wouk's major achievements as a novelist, some discussion of its technical merits seems in order.[18] Despite William Hudson's assertion that Wouk intended to focus on characterization (Hudson, 247), most readers will be caught up

in the various complications of plot that dominate the story. In its organization, the novel resembles several of Wouk's other successful ventures; *The City Boy, The Caine Mutiny*, and (later) *Inside, Outside*.
Reflecting his affection for the theater, Wouk spends considerable time
developing individual scenes, concentrating on dialogue and minute
description, with transitions between scenes often consisting of casual
explanatory paragraphs by an omniscient narrator. His method differs
from many of his other works in that Wouk chooses to tell the story in
Marjorie Morningstar almost exclusively from the vantage point of his
heroine. Rarely, until the final pages of the novel, does he describe scenes
in which she is not the center of attention. Forcing the reader to see the
world through Marjorie's eyes allows Wouk numerous occasions for
irony. Perceptive readers are more aware than the heroine of when she is
being deceived, or (more pointedly) when she is deceiving herself.
Nevertheless, through the presence of an independent narrative voice—
which at times assumes an omniscient tone—Wouk creates some distance between reader and story. Throughout, no matter how involved
readers become in Marjorie's adventure, the Trollope-like voice of the
narrator lurks in the background, emerging from time to time to offer
Olympian commentary, and reminding readers that these characters are
not realistic, but rather illustrative of larger themes: the universal story
of adolescence and young adulthood (or young Jewish adulthood, at
least).[19]

One might assume that Wouk is less concerned with his characters
than with scoring a point for conservatism. Indeed, as John Metcalf has
pointed out, the novel is filled with examples of poor plotting and characterization: "the Shapiro episode; the Airman philosophy of Hits; the
continuing naïveté of Marjorie." Nevertheless, Metcalf continues, these
unfortunate blemishes "are compensated by gratuitous excellences: the
Uncle; the wry growth of Wally Wronken; the whole, exciting smell of
youth and spring when Marjorie goes riding in Central Park with Sandy
[Goldstone]" (Metcalf, 472). I would add to this the wonderful scene in
which Marjorie and Wally spend a summer afternoon outside New York
City, and, entranced by the smell of the lilacs, share an intimate moment
capped off by an innocent kiss. Somehow, Wouk manages to escape sen-
timentalism while capturing the joy of the moment. At that instant, neither Wally nor Marjorie seems a simple cardboard cutout propped up to
illustrate any particular ideology.

How well Wouk has handled his characters throughout the novel is
open to debate. Certainly, any examination must begin with the novel's

title character. Anyone examining Wouk's career as a novelist will find only one female character comparable to Marjorie Morgenstern— Natalie Jastrow, the heroine of *Winds of War* and *War and Remembrance*. Reviewing the novel shortly after its publication, R.T. Horchler suggested that "Marjorie Morgenstern is an unworthy subject for the novelist . . . but the apparent unworthiness of his heroine is, I believe, precisely Mr. Wouk's great point" (Horchler, 123). She is, after all, only a bright daughter of an up-and-coming Jewish businessman, whose dreams of achieving fame in New York City (and perhaps beyond it) seem unrealistic, if typical of young girls her age in any generation. Nevertheless, her commonness has caused at least one critic to wonder "whether the heroine's troubles warrant quite such a large demand on" readers' attention (*TLS*, 1).

Marjorie's "struggles and desires" may be typical of "the middle-class American girl of the mid-1950s" but she is thoroughly Jewish and hence shares the benefits and limitations of that heritage (Raphael, 67). If she is, as Meyer Levin suggests, "the classic American heroine," she achieves that status only because of the "richness of her Jewish background" (Levin, 9). I am not convinced that she is American in the manner of Hester Prynne and Isabel Archer; rather, she seems to represent a certain type of American woman, caught between her dreams for self-actualization and her culture's demand that she assume a position befitting her place in that group.[20] Viewed in this light, Marjorie's pursuit of a career as an actress is particularly ironic, for this is a novel about learning one's proper role in life. For Marjorie, that role is as a wife and mother. She seems to sense that even when she is performing on the stage at Hunter College; every man in her life is a potential husband, and only rarely does she envision the possibility of abandoning marriage for a career.

The villain of the piece, Noel Airman, has been compared to a number of Hemingway heroes, and to various Byronic figures in the bohemian tradition.[21] He is, Leslie Fiedler observes, "Don Juan in the world of the bourgeoisie" (Fiedler, 69). Cynically, Fiedler remarks that it has been "Wouk's unique contribution to American letters to have identified this bugaboo of middle-class ladies with the 'Jewish intellectual' "—or, more appropriately, pseudo-intellectual (Fiedler, 257). Airman represents all that is wrong for Wouk with modernism, its simplistic solutions to eternal problems, and its overt denial of tradition. Like Tom Keefer, Airman takes the ironic stance toward life; his jaundiced approach that places self-gratification above all else makes him, in the author's eyes, most despicable. More reprehensible than Keefer, he has wasted whatever talent he might have had by refusing to work diligently at his craft. But certainly Airman's worst offense is his conscious denial of his Jewish heritage. Several reviewers and critics have referred to Noel's decision to change his name; his given name was Saul Ehrmann, and he is the son of a respected Jewish judge.[22] The special villainy of the transformation is worth noting. Like another Saul before him—but without the benefit of any incident on the road to Damascus—he abandons his Jewish name for one that is specifically Christian: Noel. Yet the name evokes other associations as well, for Airman makes it clear that he associates the name with the famous playwright, Noel Coward. The implications of both names are significant. For Noel Airman is a coward, a man running away from all of life's responsibilities. He is an Air-man, a lightweight who hides behind convenient intellectual ideologies which he only half-understands, in spite of his Ivy League education. Surely the silliness of his one original idea—his Theory of Hits—reveals the shallowness of his entire outlook. Furthermore, beneath his surface suaveness, he is an unsettled, insecure misogynist. Only a misguided adolescent would fall for such a sham; and that, of course, is exactly Marjorie's condition when she visits South Wind for the first time, at age 19. It takes her six years to learn the truth, but any reader sympathetic to her must hope that she will finally come to her senses and put aside this lightweight for someone more substantial.

Of course, the reader is led to hope that long-suffering Wally Wronken will finally "get the girl." Wally is all that Noel is not. He is a Jew who has not rejected his heritage. He works diligently to become a first-rate playwright (and eventually succeeds). He is genuinely concerned about Marjorie's feelings, and he is willing to suffer almost any ignominy to continue his relationship with the woman he loves. Wally's inability to barter his success in the theater into a marriage with Marjorie provides a note of sadness to the novel. Her blindness toward him does not fall away even when she is finally able to see Noel for what he is. Nevertheless, in the epilogue, told from Wally's point of view, the reader learns that neither he nor Marjorie has remained permanently scarred by their earlier experiences. Marjorie has conveniently managed to reconstruct her past in her own mind so as to exonerate herself for some of her more serious faux pas; Wally has found happiness in his work, and it is only in a moment of wistfulness almost two decades later that he goes to visit his old flame at her suburban home, to learn how she has fared in the intervening years. Wally's memories are like those of many well-adjusted men and women—a soft pang of regret for what was lost, a sense of bemusement about what might have been, but a concurrent appreciation for what one has achieved, with little serious desire for things to have turned out differently.

Marjorie and the Critics

The critical response to *Marjorie Morningstar* has been suggested by comments interspersed throughout the preceding discussion. It may be worthwhile, however, to review some of the more general statements made by the novel's supporters and detractors. Among the strongest supporters is John Metcalf, who considers the novel "essential reading for anyone interested in the development of transatlantic [i.e., American] writing." "What is remarkable about" the novel, Metcalf continues, is "the breadth and depth of Mr. Wouk's vision. This is novel-writing on an ample, nineteenth-century scale. The sheer professional achievement of the thing is exhilarating" (Metcalf, 270). With less lavish praise, *New York Herald Tribune* reviewer F. H. Bullock calls the work "a modern Jewish Vanity Fair . . . spacious, abundantly peopled, shrewd, observant, humane."[23] The novel's popularity can be attributed in part to the emergence of the Jewish writer from the periphery of the literary world to "the center of . . . American literature" after 1950.[24] Virtually every favorable review contains praise for Wouk's depiction of Jewish life. Earl Walbridge found that portrait "warm" and "attractive"; Nora Magid thought the "environment" both "vivid and enormously complex"; and B. R. McElderry, Jr., considered the "scenes of Jewish life" "authentic and good-natured."[25] Yet even these reviewers were not totally supportive; Magid remarks further on in her essay that "the fascinating cultural scene" is simply "backdrop" to a "banal love story" (Magid, 20).

The attacks on the novel have come from two overlapping groups: highbrow critics who panned the book's literary qualities, and members of the Jewish community who found Wouk's portrait of his religion and culture vulgar and offensive.

Among the first group, the principal charge—once again—is that the author's desire to offer moral instruction overwhelms his capacity to tell a story that illustrates his theme indirectly. A mild indictment that highlights this theme comes from reviewer R. T. Horchler: "Mr. Wouk has come to grips with serious moral and cultural questions, which he presents with knowledge and dramatic force, but not quite fairly and not in any great depth. The spokesmen for the enemy are rather too palpably

made of straw, and the resolutions to the problems are much too easy"
(Horchler, 123).

Not every critic is so gentle. Nora Magid calls the novel "a soap opera
with psychological and sociological props" (Magid, 20). Riley Hughes
judges it "incredibly vulgar . . . in a nice way, of course"; a "slick materi-
alism coats everything" in the book (Hughes, 146). The reviewer for the
New Yorker writes it off as "a damp and endless tale."[26] Norman
Podhoretz finds the novel "so obtrusively doctrinal" that it is hard to see
any literary merit in the work (Podhoretz, 186). Even a generally sympathetic critic, Joseph Cohen, believes Wouk's "formal didacticism"
"detracts from the literary achievement of his performance" (Cohen, 224).

Maxwell Geismar argues that Wouk, like W. D. Howells before him
and like his contemporary and friend John P. Marquand, is not able to
"break through the formulas which bring . . . popular success"; because
they always seem to know more than they say, and only insinuate what
they want to express, popular writers like Wouk often take an ironic
stance (Geismar, 1). Geismar finds the novel's problem to lie with this
unintentional ambiguity that leads to a sense of uncertainty; the reader is
never sure if the novel is intended as a romance or a satire. The confusion
is further complicated by Marjorie's "false emancipation"; throughout the
first half of the novel, Wouk takes pains to criticize the "petit-bourgeois
values" against which his heroine rebels, only to have her accept them—
almost cheerfully—at the end of the work (Geismar, 1).

The problem critics found with *The Caine Mutiny* is also present here:
Wouk appears to want to revel in the excesses of liberalism while ultimately championing conservative values. As he does in his sea novel,
Wouk provides an end reversal that seems to vitiate his arguments in the
main body of the work: the "sudden reversal near the end, the injection
of conservative values in a manner which is structurally weak and at
odds with the character values established" earlier in the novel bothers
B. R. McElderry (McElderry, 133). Allen Guttmann presents the dilemma succinctly: "The novel's last hundred pages nail down the thesis that
religiously observant middle-class domesticity is better than the dream
of Romantic love, only to have Wally Wronken pop up with the notion
that the dream lingers on . . . Perhaps he, like Wouk, wants to have it
both ways" (Guttmann, 123). Ultimately, as B. R. McElderry notes,
Wouk is "a conservative in disguise. No matter what he lets the young
people say and do . . . it is the older generation that is right." Though
Wouk has great talent, his adherence to the conservative position "has

forced him into strained, awkward, and unconvincing patterns of fiction" (McElderry, 137, 135–36).

Norman Podhoretz thinks Wouk is simply cheating his readers: "[The novel] gives its audience a satisfied sense of having grappled with difficult questions, of having made an honest, painstaking effort to examine both sides of a problem before reaching a mature decision." It is actually dishonest, however; the real problems with "the kind of Judaism which involves dietary laws and certain other observances" are simply not recognized as problems for real-life Jews trying to make their lives in real-life America (Podhoretz, 186). As if that stinging denouncement were not enough, Podhoretz goes on to castigate Wouk's handling of his craft: "Utterly incapable of rendering the feel of an emotion or a conversation, he points vaguely into space like a blind man trying to locate an object in an unfamiliar room" (Podhoretz, 186).

Negative criticism is always unpleasant for the writer, but having a judgment such as Podhoretz's printed in the prestigious Jewish periodical *Commentary* must have been especially hard for Wouk to take. Other Jewish publications were not much kinder. Writing in 1959, Joseph Cohen reported that it was "a widely known fact that *Marjorie Morningstar* has been received with hostility and bitterness by the American Jewish press and among the spiritual leaders in the American Jewish community." Cohen believes the harsh criticism stems from what is perceived to be "Wouk's somewhat naturalistic travesty of the Jewish character, holidays, and ceremonies" (Cohen, 221–22). The feelings persist in some quarters; as late as 1984, Marc Lee Raphael was writing in *American Jewish History* that the novel was little more than "an assemblage of stereotypes—most of negative, indifferent, and ignorant Jews"; its final 20 pages did little to "meliorate the Jewish wasteland of the Morgensterns" (Raphael, 66–67).[27]

Nevertheless, as Raphael remarks, "while rabbis from their pulpits denounced as libelous [the novel's] fierce criticism of Jewish life, the American public bought thousands of copies each week" (Raphael, 67). The "inside" of Jewish life—a life unknown to many Americans, who distrusted Jews for irrational causes—was made vivid and understandable to millions. Even Norman Podhoretz concedes that "Marjorie is after all a Jewish girl," and *Marjorie Morningstar* may be "the first novel to treat American Jews intimately as Jews without making them seem exotic" (Podhoretz, 188). Whatever its literary defects, its popular success signalled for at least one critic an important watershed in American sociology: it is "the first fictional celebration of the mid-twentieth-century detente between Jews and middle-class America" (Fiedler, 258). The distinguished editors of *The Rise of American Jewish Literature*, Meyer Levin and Charles Angoff, observe in their introduction that "*Marjorie Morningstar* really catapulted interest in Jewish material to a lofty high."[28] Instead of being shunted as outsiders, Jewish writers and Jewish people now had a place in American literature. Their experience was no longer considered occult or marginal. After *Marjorie Morningstar*, Marc Raphael says, Jewish writers, "once the strangers within the gates," have found that they can "use their past to interpret America to Americans, to create and shape the images by which Americans define themselves" (Raphael, 72). In this sense, Wouk is precursor to the great Jewish novelists of the later decades: Philip Roth, Bernard Malamud, Saul Bellow—no small accomplishment for someone who simply wanted to tell a story about a young girl growing up and falling in love.

Back to the Theatre

Immediately following his success with *Marjorie Morningstar*, Wouk turned his talents once again to the stage, writing a comic farce titled *Nature's Way*. He details the haphazard life of a young couple in New York, experiencing the natural tribulations of newlyweds: petty discomfort at having to adjust to each other, gentle suspicions that having given up the freedom of single life might not have been the best choice. The husband, a composer, is struggling to complete a new work to ward off income-tax difficulties; his librettist friend (who is actually upset by the marriage and tries throughout the performance to separate the couple) takes him on a European holiday, fueling his wife's concerns about his fidelity. The plot is complicated by the presence of the wife's mother, who has difficulty understanding how her daughter, though married for only four months, can be six months pregnant. The comedy tends toward slapstick for most of the play, as the young lovers overcome the sinister friend and doubting mother-in-law to convince each other that their love is genuine.

Nature's Way opened on Broadway on 16 October 1957. Despite a strong cast that included comics Orson Bean and Betsy von Fuerstenberg and personalities on the brink of fame such as Beatrice Arthur and Godfrey Cambridge, it ran for only 61 performances. Wouk surely realized that this could not be considered a success, especially when compared with the long run *The Caine Mutiny Court-Martial* had enjoyed. No "single real enthusiast" emerged from among the opening-night reviewers.[29] Critics panned it as simply another attempt to achieve commercial success by pandering to the general public's naturally conservative tastes. Tom Driver, writing in *Christian Century*, suggested that Wouk was trying to be "the new spokesman for virtue," wishing to "spread propaganda for marriage, chastity, and the begetting of children" while satirizing "urban sophistication, homosexuality, and natural childbirth."[30] There is satire, but it is not stinging enough; hence, the play simply meanders through a series of diatribes, never becoming too vitriolic to offend playgoers who may admire what Wouk despises, and who have invested good money to see the performance.[31] It is doubtful if Wouk was too hurt by any of these barbs, since by the time the play closed, he was immersed in what was to be for him a much more serious project.

Youngblood Hawke

Wouk began *Youngblood Hawke* on 18 October 1957, the day *Nature's Way* opened on Broadway. He spent four years working intermittently on the novel, interrupting his effort to compose his only extended piece of nonfiction, *This Is My God*, a treatise on Judaism that appeared in 1959. During the novel's gestation, Wouk moved his family to the Virgin Islands. All of this peripheral information may not have much to do with the work's mixed success, but there is a strong possibility that disruptions in his work schedule, coupled with his choice of a somewhat unfamiliar subject, may have contributed to Wouk's inability to bring off the success he no doubt envisioned for this massive work.

For *Youngblood Hawke* is indeed massive: almost 900 pages of closely printed text, it is longer than any of Wouk's works except *Winds of War* and *War and Remembrance*. The hero, a burly Kentuckian who emerges from coalmining country with a prodigious appetite for hard work and an unusual ability to spin yarns about the American heartland and American history, comes to New York City to find a publisher for a collection of novels that he is sure will secure his place as the outstanding writer of the century. He is befriended by a demure editor, Jeanne Green, who shepherds his first novel through the press. Success quickly attracts a following in the publishing industry, however, and Hawke soon finds himself embroiled in a romance with New York socialite Frieda Winter (another suggestive name), and caught up in various schemes to increase his fortune and avoid losing all his newfound wealth to the tax collector. At the same time, he tries to help his mother, who is having money problems as she attempts to settle a mining claim in the Hawkes' hometown of Hovey, Kentucky. There, Hawke's unscrupulous cousin tries simultaneously to swindle Mrs. Hawke out of her money and get Arthur (the novelist's real name) to invest in various shopping center schemes. In both his amorous and his business affairs, Hawke strives to keep alive his artistic spirit and preserve his integrity as a writer. The effort finally kills him.

Critics were not long in noticing the strong similarities between Wouk's protagonist and the southern writer Thomas Wolfe. The remarkable parallels in their careers caused many critics to protest in outrage at what more than one called an "act of violence" done to the life of one of the South's most gifted and tragic authors. The reviewer for *Time* magazine carped that "Wouk has borrowed almost everything from Wolfe but his cufflinks."[32] Nevertheless, a number of more perceptive reviewers noted that Hawke was actually "a composite of Wolfe and Wouk, with Wolfe's background and ferocious energy, and Wouk's practicality."[33] Charles Angoff remarked that Wouk's portrayal of a character so akin to the legendary Wolfe displayed a "desire to identify" with the novelist whose life mirrored the romantic art he captured so powerfully in his fiction (Levin and Agnoff, 512). As another critic noted, a strong resemblance exists between "the type of novels Hawke turns out and those that (since the publication of *The Caine Mutiny*) have made Herman Wouk the most successful fiction writer, commercially speaking, of his generation" (Dempsey, 1). Somehow, by writing so detailed an account of such a figure, Wouk was living out a fantasy he was unable to realize in his own life, where the demands of family and religion kept him close to home, faithful to his wife, and focused on earning a decent living for his dependents. This novel, perhaps more than any of his others, allowed Wouk to use fiction for the time-honored purposes of escapism and role-playing. If Allen Guttmann is correct, it also afforded Wouk a revenge on his critics: this novel, Guttmann argues, dramatizes Wouk's "annoyance with the negative critical reaction to his commercially successful works" (Guttmann 123–24).

Unquestionably, Wouk has a serious theme to pursue in *Youngblood Hawke*: the tragedy of wasted talents. "Here," critic David Dempsey remarks, "is the urgent theme that has so often haunted the American success story—the wasting of power that tragically becomes the price of great achievement" (Dempsey, 1). In this novel, Wouk surveys, if episodically, the impact of the business world on the creative novelist. Hawke arrives in New York hoping to make money but still infused with an ide-

alism about writing that drives him to spend the wee hours of every
morning slaving over his material to shape works of art that will live into
the next century. By the novel's end, he is spending those same hours
cranking out pages that he hopes will outlast the next publication of the
New York Times best-seller list. In a sense, the novel is "a portrait of the
artist as big businessman," and a tragic one at that.[34] The novel's
strength lies in Wouk's ability to display the shallowness of the publishing world that cares little for artistic integrity; as long as a work will sell,
the artist remains a prized thoroughbred in the publisher's stable. While
a number of critics dismissed the work as simply "a costume novel of the
publishing industry" (Boroff, 10), some have suggested that its immediate subject is a metaphor for an even more pervasive illness in American
society. "This novel" Stanley Kauffmann comments, "is a microcosm of
our time, an unwitting biopsy of the social body that reveals monetary
malignancy" (Kauffmann, 24).

The reaction of the American reading public was predictably favorable. The novel rose to the top of the best-seller lists, was selected by
Book-of-the-Month Club, and appeared in paperback. It was eventually
made into a movie starring James Franciscus in the title role, and featuring Suzanne Pleshette, Genevieve Page, Eva Gabor, and Mary Astor—
all recognized names in the film industry.[35] Reviewers for popular
periodicals and newspapers found it "a warmhearted, sentimental story,"
"a clever novel" in which Wouk exhibits once again his "rare gift" as a
"natural storyteller." One finds in the plot an "inner consistency and sustained imagination which brings a remarkable plausibility to his tale of
Gargantuan fiscal folly and supersophisticated romance." Another goes
so far as to suggest that the work would "have stunned even Dickens"—
a sincere compliment. The novel is "quite convincing to anyone who has
been close to the Manhattan scene." Even less exuberant reviewers
admitted that Wouk "triumphs over his own ineptitude and carries the
reader along in a strong narrative flow"; though one of Wouk's supporters is bold enough to suggest that his method "risks little beyond the
story it serves," and that the novelist "has yet to make the final leap into
his art."[36]

In general, though, the novel has been judged a critical failure. Three
areas are most often cited as weak points: weak characterization, episod-
ic plotting, and an overbearing tendency on the author's part to use his
characters to preach at his readers. Each point deserves some attention,
since these failures are often cited to deny Wouk a place among the best
novelists of this century.

Though some critics insisted that, even in *Youngblood Hawke*, Wouk is "just about the best portrayer of people in action on the current literary horizon" (*Tribune*, 4), few who reviewed the novel upon publication or since have praised Wouk's handling of his characters. The critical consensus is that the people in *Youngblood Hawke* are "pasteboard characters," "cereal-box cutouts" who are "constructed with the knit-browed, honest concentration of a child working with a Meccano set."[37] Perhaps the most damning indictments have been leveled at the title character. "I have found it easier to believe in Hawke's financial manipulations than I do in his writing," the reviewer for *Atlantic Monthly* observed.[38] He "never comes alive at his writing desk, which is the normal center of a novelist's life" (*Tribune*, 4). Hawke's business bunglings in the publishing industry, and his affairs with the various women who wander in and out of his life are of most interest to the reader, because Wouk focuses our attention on them. Wouk may not see the business of writing as worthy of his readers' attention. Certainly if he thinks that all writers work as he does—pencils sharpened and ready on his desk every day, pads of yellow note paper neatly stacked for the four to six hours he will spend composing placidly in the quiet of his study—then he may be right. Like Anthony Trollope, whose methodical composition process has become legendary in the literary world, Wouk is a writer who equates composition with activities such as accounting. No doubt he feels the excitement of creativity as he composes; but when he turned to writing about a character much like himself, he either chose to ignore this key element, or was unable to bring that excitement to life. *Youngblood Hawke* is less believable for this omission or failure. Worse, in this novel Wouk fails to make other characters convincing or lifelike. As one reviewer observed, the novel's men and women "enlist halfhearted sympathy. If the author doesn't care, why should we?"[39] When one considers the compelling portraits in *The Caine Mutiny*, this charge cannot be applied to all of Wouk's fiction, but it does explain *Youngblood Hawke*'s failure to achieve the critical status of other novels in the Wouk canon.

To make matters worse, Wouk failed to shape the disparate plot lines into a coherent narrative. Described by one critic as a "huge, ungainly novel," *Youngblood Hawke* moves episodically at a ponderous pace, rather than with any controlling direction.[40] Wouk seems insistent on including as many details as possible about the business life (and love life) of the successful novelist, and as a result readers sense that they are watching a play in which characters keep wandering across the stage without any particular justification. This may resemble life, but art should be more controlled. Among the novel's intrinsic weaknesses, David Boroff notes, is its "remorseless prolixity" (Boroff, 36). It is, in Stanley Hyman's view, "783 pages of the most desperate contrivance" (Hyman, 69)—in marked contrast to Wolfe's spontaneous creative outbursts. Remarking on Jeanne Green's editing of Hawke's manuscripts, reminiscent of Maxwell Perkins's editing of the prolix Thomas Wolfe, Simon Raven asks: "Where was Mr. Wouk's editor when this novel was printing?"[41]

As if such criticisms were not serious enough, there is even more damning commentary about Wouk's handling of theme and techniques of presentation. He "tends to overwrite," a contemporary reviewer wrote, and "occasionally to sermonize," and he "sometimes borders on the histrionic" (Simon, 1919). He has "spelt everything out," another remarked, "so solemnly and massively that the book proceeds, as it were, in slow motion" (Raven, 600). Others have noted that "the style, at its highest moments, is commonplace" (Kauffmann, 24), and that the author "descends into triteness and oversentimentality."[42] "A certain profundity, an enriching universality" to augment the storyline is missing (Guidry, 7). Stanley Kauffman's opinions are the most damning of all. "What is chiefly depressing about this novel," he says, is that "it rests on a base of horrible, suffocating sincerity. . . . The ideas that are expressed are the utterances of a tapioca mind" (Kauffmann, 24). Not every reader would agree with Stanley Hyman's assessment of the novel, but it is worth citing as a final commentary on *Youngblood Hawke*. "Is there nothing good about the book? Nothing. It is the most fraudulent and worthless novel I have read in many years" (Hyman, 70).

I have dwelt on this negative criticism for two reasons. First, because it can be justified by a reading of the text. Also, while one can argue that *Youngblood Hawke* is better than these critics have indicated, too many qualities are lacking for the novel to be regarded as a serious literary work. Had Wouk set out simply to tell a story about the publishing industry and to poke fun at its excesses—as he does with the advertising industry in *Aurora Dawn*—criticism might be less warranted. There is a seriousness of purpose to *Youngblood Hawke* that requires that the work be judged as both a literary artifact and a social statement. While Wouk's views about the callousness of the trade may be granted, he cannot be excused for poor characterization, inferior plotting, wooden dialogue (an infrequently cited fault, but one obvious throughout the novel), or a tendency to resort to oratory inappropriate to the circumstances.

Nevertheless, some of the criticism seems unduly vitriolic, and appears motivated by something other than pure critical examination. Wouk is, after all, a self-professed social critic, and like his other novels, *Youngblood Hawke* is an attempt to expose an area of American society that was in need of reform. Wouk may have chosen Wolfe as a model because he saw the spark of genius in that writer's fiction somehow perverted by the establishment. In Wouk's view, Wolfe may have become a "modernist" writer not by choice, but at the prompting of those for whom he worked. If the novel is a criticism of the power of money to corrupt, and an exposé of the liberal viewpoint as it undermines traditional American values, then it demands attention for that reason alone. Arnold Beichman may be right in suggesting that Wouk has been taken to task more for his conservative views than for any technical faux pas he has committed.[43] Nevertheless, many faults in the novel's construction suggest that Wouk did not succeed in creating a work of literature capable of carrying his social message.

This Is My God

The disjointedness that characterizes *Youngblood Hawke* may be due to the fact that the author's attention was divided during the composition process. Wouk interrupted his work on the novel to compose his only extended piece of nonfiction, *This Is My God*, a mixture of analysis and anecdote published by Simon & Schuster in 1959 and serialized in the *New York Herald Tribune*. In it, Wouk offers an explanation for Orthodox Judaism, making no excuses for the many harsh rules which characterize that religion. The scope is limited—Wouk confesses that he is "wholly unequipped to discuss either Christianity or Islam"—but in over 200 pages Wouk deals respectfully with the external trappings that set his chosen form of worship apart from other religions in American society. *This Is My God* is not intended as a religious textbook; rather, Wouk addresses a larger, non-Jewish audience, not to convert them to his faith but simply to make them understand why Orthodox Jews behave and believe as they do. Not surprisingly, with his "unerring instinct for reaching the general reader," Wouk succeeded in attaining an unusually large readership, even for a work with a subject that might be thought to make many American readers uncomfortable.[44] Reviewers found this "eloquent, personal cry for Orthodoxy" a "warm, readable, and admirably clear account of the fundamentals of the Jewish faith" that was highly successful because Wouk managed to "steer clear of some of the common faults which frequently mar works of this subject area—the tendency to oversimplify; the tendency to become either too strident or too patronizing in tone."[45]

Yet even this book had its critics, especially among the Orthodox Jewish community. Many found the account too simplistic, believing that Wouk had mistaken accidents of behavior for the substance of belief. Will Herberg, writing in the *New York Times Book Review*, suggested that while the book made "no concession of essentials for the sake of popularity," Wouk's method of presentation was "too relaxed" and too focused on externals; its "failure to focus the attention of the reader upon the inner reality of faith" was its "most serious shortcoming."[46] In his *Midstream* review, Robert Gordis accused Wouk of "oversimplification" and a "failure to explore the fundamental implications of his own position." Gordis faults Wouk for not facing up squarely to the way traditions are passed down through generations (Wouk and his grandfather belong to different worlds, Gordis points out), and for presenting Judaism as "a single monolithic structure," ignoring "the multicolored variety to be found even within the purview of Orthodox Jewry" (Gordis, 89).

Despite this criticism, however, *This Is My God* seems to have been a success. Wouk set out to reach a wide audience and provide an introduction to his faith. While that explanation may be simplistic—especially to members of the Orthodox faith who have grown up understanding the nuances of their belief—the text did much to make the practices of Orthodox Jews intelligible to an American society where pluralism and laissez-faire are the watchwords of religious observance. Even a casual reading reveals the loving attention that Wouk lavished on this tribute to his heritage. Many of the biographical details currently available about the novelist are scattered throughout this work. His passion for order and discipline, his belief that conservatism and a commitment to tradition are essential for any society's survival, come through strongly. Perhaps more than any other of his works, *This Is My God* serves as a coda for Wouk's beliefs about human nature and social relationships. It is an ideological guidebook to his fiction.

Don't Stop the Carnival

Unfortunately, this fine volume of nonfiction is overshadowed by the two novels that immediately followed it. Despite its commercial success,

Youngblood Hawke added little to Wouk's critical stature. His next novel, *Don't Stop the Carnival*, threatened to destroy Wouk's reputation as a popular novelist as well. Though it made the best-seller lists (as might be expected for any of Wouk's novels by this point in his career), even ardent Wouk supporters received it with dismay. Its setting is the island of Amerigo, a fictionalized version of St. Thomas in the Virgin Islands, where Wouk had been living since 1958. The hero, Norman Paperman, is a middle-aged Jewish New Yorker, who has decided to abandon fast-paced Manhattan for a more sedate climate and lifestyle in the Caribbean. Paperman buys a hotel on Amerigo and sets out to make his fortune there. As one might expect, things do not go as smoothly as the hero hopes. Trusted employees quit; nothing works at the hotel, and no one seems to be able to fix the broken machinery. Paperman becomes enamored of a former movie star, who turns out to be the mistress of the island's governor. His principal financial backer abandons him. Naturally, however, Wouk manages to bring things to a successful close, as Paperman finally overcomes obstacles and manages to fix both the hotel's structure and finances. Only the accidental death of the movie star and the murder of a local businessman mar the idyllic scene. Since these events occur before the grand carnival that serves as the book's climax, it is easy for readers to dismiss them as merely unpleasant.

Among the few reviewers who found something to praise in the novel, the *New York Times* critic called it a "clock-racingly readable" account of "a new America, freed, like the old, from British rule," with Wouk's hero a kind of Adam thrust into an Edenic setting to make a new life for himself and his family.[47] Others strained for something good to say. One noted that individual scenes, especially comic ones, come alive in this work as in other Wouk novels.[48] Another remarked that, once again, Wouk had managed to place this novel "close to the center of contemporary middle-class American experience" (Buitenhuis, 47).

The general opinion was far from laudatory. Even critics usually sympathetic to Wouk had to admit that, while the novel might be entertaining, it was "not vintage Wouk." Its Caribbean setting "has surface attractions," but "for the rest, it is matter for compulsive readers." Wouk's "murky, modern, antiromantic intelligence" vitiates the sense of enchantment promised by the setting and plot; the novel has a pervading sense of irony that makes it unsettling reading.[49] Samuel Simon, who had good things to say about other Wouk novels, found this one "trite and unconvincing." "Anyone who has read Herman Wouk's previous books knows that he has the talent to write satisfying fiction,"

Simon wrote. It is especially disappointing that he is responsible for what Simon considers "a shoddy and absurd novel."[50]

The faults lie in three areas: plotting, characterization, and a lack of clear focus that results in a dishonest portrayal of moral values. The plot came under direct attack from reviewers who found it "wearying" as "disaster after disaster" turns the hero's island paradise into "hell on earth." The "repeated stories of mishaps" pile up "towards boredom," making the novel "superficial and unrewarding." "There is a plenitude of incident in the novel," this same critic continued, "and abundance of characters"; unfortunately, neither is brought into focus.[51]

Regarding characterization, the *Christian Science Monitor*'s critic likened his experience in plodding through *Don't Stop the Carnival* to "climbing into an overnight bus, too full of people sleeping too long." All of Wouk's skill as a novelist "cannot dispel a smog of joyless pleasure that hangs over his characters as drearily as much-breathed air."[52] Haskel Frankel saw Wouk's hero living in "a land of labels" (quoted in Charney, 386). The reviewer for the *New Statesman* cited the narrator's observation that "life in Kinja {the natives' name for Amerigo} teetered always between the dreadful and the ridiculous" and observed, "So does the book. Mr. Wouk invents the kind of characters one sees only in B-films."[53] Mark Charney judged it "replete with type characters and predictable situations" (Charney, 386).

Clearly the novel lacks character development. The opinion of Wouk's friend Arnold Beichman, that Norman Paperman "is one of the most fully realized characters in the Wouk oeuvre" and that Iris Tramm demonstrates Wouk's ability to create "highly credible and fascinating female characters" is a minority judgment (Beichman, 34, 35–36). Wouk spends little time examining motivation for any of his characters—even his hero, Norman Paperman, is given thin, almost implausible motives for abandoning his life as a New York advertising executive for the shimmering beaches of Kinja. Only facile explanations are offered for the behavior of men and women in self-imposed exile on his Caribbean paradise. No one has any substance or complexity; they are comic, or erotic, or self-centered, to a degree that one seldom finds in real life. That the book is intended as comedy helps explain some of Wouk's reticence to delve deeply into his characters' inner lives. But if that is an excuse, it is also reason to dismiss the work as mere entertainment, and not the penetrating look at middle-class values that some scenes and conversations suggest.

Worse, some reviewers believed that Wouk revels in describing, even condoning, the rather immoral lifestyles of the inhabitants of Amerigo. In what one described as "going even further than necessary to pander to his market" (Buitenhuis, 47), Wouk spends considerable time relating the sexual indiscretions of his characters, excusing their behavior by appealing to clichés of island life, vacations, or the need to find respite from the trials of American success. This, Peter Buitenhuis remarks, "is an artificially spontaneous, immorally moral version of life that contains the best warning against itself in its own title. If you stop the carnival for one minute and start thinking about it, the book collapses in a welter of false values" (Buitenhuis, 47). A final damning comment by Haskel Frankel, delivered with more genuine playfulness and irony than most scenes in the novel itself, sums up the general reaction to this work: "If a novel can be both thin and heavy, *Don't Stop the Carnival* is that novel—more Wouk than play, and that makes a dull buy" (Frankel, 128).

The legion of Wouk detractors among highbrow critics no doubt saw *Don't Stop the Carnival* as yet another sign that Wouk was simply a commercial parasite on the body of the American reading public. Unfortunately, even sympathetic readers may have begun to wonder if this novel might be a signal that Wouk had indeed lost his powers of imagination and his gift for strong plots and subtle characters. The strengths of insight that had made *The Caine Mutiny* and, to a lesser extent, *Marjorie Morningstar*, minor classics in popular American publishing, are not in evidence here. Fortunately, as he was finishing *Don't Stop the Carnival*, Wouk decided that it was time to return to a subject that had been with him for years: that great human catastrophe, the Second World War. In *The Caine Mutiny*, he had only scratched its surface; there was much more to examine, much more to say. So, in 1964, Wouk relocated his family to Washington, D.C., taking up residence in fashionable Georgetown so that he could be closer to the people and the documents that he would need to begin work on the project that he hoped would gain him lasting fame among American novelists.

Chapter Five

Exploring the Causes and Consequences of War

Developing a Historical Romance

Arnold Beichman reports that Wouk once noted in his journals that he considered *The Caine Mutiny, Marjorie Morningstar*, and *Youngblood Hawke* to be experimental vehicles for him to develop his powers as a novelist.[1] If so, then we must assume that they were preparatory to the work on which Wouk was to spend nearly two decades: an investigation of the causes and consequences of the greatest conflagration in history, World War II. Beichman notes that Wouk began outlining *The Winds of War* on 17 May 1962, the day *Youngblood Hawke* was published. It would be Wouk's most ambitious project, occupying him for 16 years, as his exploration of America's involvement in World War II, and the effects of war on the United States, Europe, and Asia, would grow to two volumes of fiction, each over 1,000 pages long. The novelist actually began writing *The Winds of War* in 1965; this prelude to the Japanese attack on Pearl Harbor was published in 1971. Seven years later, the second volume, *War and Remembrance*, appeared on American booksellers' shelves (Beichman 17, 19, 20n). Like many of Wouk's earlier novels, these works were picked up by book clubs and were gobbled up by avid readers; sales zoomed into the millions.[2]

Research for his study of World War II took Wouk back to naval facilities, to the Library of Congress, to Minsk in Russia, to Siena, Warsaw, London, Lisbon, Moscow, Yalta, Berlin—even to Auschwitz—to talk to people and assimilate the ambiance of locations he would use in his narrative.[3] He moved to Georgetown in 1964 so he could be closer to the people he needed to visit and the documents he needed to review to assure the historical accuracy of his work. So committed was he to completing what he considered to be his magnum opus, that in 1972 he rented a hideaway in Middleburg, Virginia, west of Washington so he could work on *War and Remembrance* with fewer interruptions.[4]

The scope of the work seems overwhelming at first. As a critic in the prestigious *Political Science Quarterly* remarked with understatement, "World War II is the subject" of this "1900-page, two-volume work," which "falls somewhere between fiction and history."[5] Wouk himself has been careful to categorize the work as a historical romance, to distinguish it from the historical novel.[6] The distinction is important to literary scholars and historians, since writers of romance are usually accorded greater latitude in rearranging historical events and engaging in fantasy than either historians or historical novelists, who claim to offer realistic portraits of people and events, using fictional characters to emphasize the effects of history on everyday people.[7] The method, "invented" by Sir Walter Scott near the beginning of the nineteenth century, has served writers well, for fiction often provides more opportunities for exploring human tragedy and triumph than the scholarly narrative of the historian. According to one critic (a political scientist by training), Wouk's books "give more vivid pictures of the principal leaders of the war than military and political history could" because "fiction is better than history at showing 'how it really was' where matters of human character are concerned" (Mandelbaum, 517).

Though during the 1970s and 1980s, novelists have increasingly turned to the Vietnam conflict when writing about war, as late as 1983 sociologist Karen McPherson could comment that "writers of military fiction still look largely to World War II for their inspiration and for their metaphors of valor and courage that are associated with warfare."[8] Wouk, seasoned and matured by his own experiences in that war, naturally returned to it to capture his own understanding of what has happened to American society as a result of WWII, and its subsequent emergence as a world power.

Plotting and Peopling a World at War

Despite his claim that the work is merely a romance, Wouk does not simply wish to describe what happened to America and the world from 1938 to 1945. He wants to make a strong statement about the nature of his country and the men and women who serve it in times of crisis; he also wants to say something about the lunacy of modern warfare and the need for a new world order in which the preservation of peace is paramount in the minds of those who control the fate of nations.

This is quite a tall order for any book, but Wouk takes it on cheerfully in his sprawling narrative. Unlike most war novels, which focus on either small groups of common soldiers or sailors, or which examine the pressures of the conflict as felt by those in charge of grand strategy, *The Winds of War* and *War and Remembrance* provide a sweeping look at all aspects of the conflagration. Wouk constructs a complex tale of the great and the small as they try to deal with the madness unleashed on the world by Adolph Hitler.

"Wouk's method," observes Richard Bolton, author of an extensive analysis of *The Winds of War*, "is to be a good storyteller," avoiding "stylistic experiments," "time manipulation," and "flights of allegory"—techniques that Bolton says might have endeared Wouk to academic critics. "Through style," Bolton continues, "Wouk seeks first to capture the reader's attention and imagination, then to influence his perceptions and values."[9] "Wouk's large design," Pearl Bell says, is "to dramatize both the nobility and the horror of World War II by means of the tragic experiences endured by one ordinary, typical American Family."[10] What he wishes to create, in short, is an American epic on the scale of Homer's *Iliad* or Virgil's *Aeneid*: the story of a nation struggling for its very life, and the tale of the hero (or in Wouk's case, heroes) whose noble actions bring glory to themselves and their people.

Any attempt to detail the plot of this sprawling story would occupy nearly half a small critical volume. Wouk actually uses a series of plot lines running parallel and intersecting at various points along the way. Generally, the two novels trace the history of the Henrys, a navy family caught up in the war in rather intricate ways as choice and circumstance place one or more of them at the focal point of almost every major event between the prewar years and the conflict's climax in 1945. A character sketch of the main fictional personages may help illuminate the complex plot and shed some light on Wouk's method of composition as well as his aims in writing both novels.

Wouk's hero is Victor "Pug" Henry, a career naval officer who in 1938 accepts assignment to Berlin as a naval attaché because he thinks his career is coming to a close. His astute observations about Germany's readiness for war come to the attention of President Franklin Roosevelt, who decides to use Henry as an unofficial observer and envoy on a number of missions to Germany, England, Russia, and the Middle East throughout the war. In the course of these assignments, he meets all the world leaders and manages to be present at a number of significant events, such as the bombing of London, the Allied air raids on Germany, and the siege of Leningrad. Henry never gives up his dream of commanding a battleship, even when he is travelling the globe on assignment from the White House or working in Washington on landing craft projects. Though the Japanese sink the battleship he was to command in their attack on Pearl Harbor, Henry does become skipper of the cruiser USS *Northampton*, allowing him to participate at Midway and other, lesser naval engagements in the Pacific. During the course of the novel he is promoted first to naval captain, then to admiral; at the Battle of Leyte Gulf he commands a battleship division. Henry ends his naval career as aide to President Harry Truman.

Henry, former Naval Academy football player, who is still trim and fit for battle at age 50, is Wouk's symbol of the military professional. He possesses what Bolton describes as "that combination of traits the Romans called *gravitas*—patience, stamina, responsibility, judgment" (Bolton, 400–1). He becomes "the confidant" of "presidents and prime ministers" (*WR*, 248) because he has what Franklin Roosevelt calls "a knack for putting things clearly" (*WR*, 589). His very name, as Bolton points out, signals his purpose in the novel: he is a victor of kingly proportions (Bolton, 392). (The significance of "Henry" is a bit more obscure, but it has been the name of numerous rulers of both England and France over the centuries.) Further, he says at an early point in the novel that he is an American of French and English descent (*WW*, 194)—a living embodiment of the Alliance that defeated Hitler.[11]

A man does not serve a naval career alone, and Wouk uses the novel to explore the relationships between Pug and his family. Rhoda, his wife of more than two decades, becomes disenchanted with navy life, and engages in more than one extramarital affair while her husband is off fighting for their country. Both of her lovers, electrical engineer Palmer Kirby and Army Colonel Harrison Peters, are involved in developing the country's super-secret weapon that will eventually end the war.

Pug Henry is not left alone, however. Early in *The Winds of War* he meets a young British woman, Pamela Tudsbury, daughter of a famous correspondent. The two cross paths several times during the next seven years, and in the process fall in love—an innocent love, as Pug remains faithful to his wife until he is convinced that she is leaving him. Pamela's dogged pursuit of the American naval officer ends with their marriage after Rhoda has divorced Victor to marry Harrison Peters.

The three Henry children also have roles to play. Eldest son Warren, who like his father is a graduate of the U.S. Naval Academy, goes to flight school, marries the daughter of one of America's leading isolationists in the United States Senate, and is eventually killed at Midway. Madeline, the only daughter and youngest child, takes advantage of the new freedom she discovers when the war causes their family to move off in different directions, overseas and to various military bases. She moves to New York, takes up with a despicable radio talk show host, eventually comes to her senses, marries a young naval officer who is drafted by Dr. Robert Oppenheimer to work on the Manhattan project, and lands in New Mexico with her husband at the time of the first test of the atomic bomb.

The Henrys' middle child, Byron, is a reluctant warrior, and through him Wouk introduces his second major theme, the effect of the war on the Jewish people. When *The Winds of War* opens, Byron is in Italy working as a researcher for distinguished American scholar Aaron Jastrow, a Jew who has written a popular study of Christ called *A Jew's Jesus*.[12] Jastrow's niece Natalie, also a researcher, falls for Byron as he does for her, though she is already involved with Leslie Slote, a U.S. State Department official. Byron and Natalie visit Slote in Warsaw just as the Germans invade Poland, the first of many difficulties they encounter. Byron, a naval reservist, is pressed by his father to return to the United States to go to submarine school, while Natalie remains in Italy with her uncle. Problems with his passport cause Aaron Jastrow difficulties with the Germans, and both he and Natalie find themselves detained behind enemy lines. Though Byron is able to meet Natalie briefly in Lisbon and marry her there during three wonderful days of romance and lovemaking, he cannot convince her to leave her uncle and return to America. As a result, their son Louis, conceived during the honeymoon, is born behind enemy lines; eventually Aaron, Natalie (unable to escape despite her American citizenship), and Louis are hauled across the continent as prisoners of the Nazis. They spend some time in Theresienstadt, the "model camp" faked by the Nazis to fool visitors from the International Red Cross, and are finally shipped to Auschwitz, where Aaron is gassed and Natalie barely escapes death, freed at the last moment by the Allies. While the Jastrows are dragged across Europe, Byron serves aboard a submarine in the Pacific, eventually rising to command a boat and distinguishing himself through his heroism in times of crisis.

As one might expect in a romance (as opposed to a realistic novel), Wouk has his hero perform a number of acts that materially affect the outcome of the war. For example, Pug Henry receives orders directly from Roosevelt to assemble a large number of fighter planes—officially designated "surplus" but really first-line aircraft—to ferry to Britain as part of Lend-Lease. At another point, Henry steps in at a critical moment to convince Stalin to release information about Russian harbors so the Americans can bring much-needed supplies to the Soviets. Later, his diplomacy is critical in getting the Soviets to publicize the help Americans have been giving them through Lend-Lease. Such literary license is balanced throughout, however, by the author's repeated interjections of what might be called straight historical narrative, in which he provides detailed and highly accurate information about the course of the war.

Richard Bolton suggests that "Wouk is concerned not only with re-creating and interpreting World War II, but . . . with advancing his own moral views of the society and world to which that war gave rise" (Bolton, 399). To accomplish these aims, Wouk devises an intricate plot which advances more than half-a-dozen fictional stories, a brief philosophical analysis of the war (provided in the form of a fictional diary by scholar Aaron Jastrow), and two distinct historical accounts of the war's progress. Though the seven divisions of the story seem a bit arbitrary, Wouk is able to maintain readers' interest in all of his characters through a careful balance between stories, reminiscent of nineteenth-century novelists and their multi-plot sagas. Over the course of 2,000 pages, Wouk interweaves accounts of Pug Henry's growing estrangement from his wife; Rhoda's various affairs with Palmer Kirby and Harrison Peters; Warren Henry's romance with and marriage to Janice Lacouture; Madeline Henry's fling in New York with radio mogul Hugh Cleveland and her eventual marriage to Simon Anderson; Byron Henry's pursuit of Natalie Jastrow, and his attempts to free his wife and infant son from the clutches of the Nazis; Natalie's flight from the Nazis with her uncle Aaron, and their sojourns in various concentration and death camps; and Pug's curious romance with Pamela Tudsbury.[13]

Wouk uses several different narrative voices over the course of the work. The most common is an omniscient fictional narrator, dispassionate and reportorial, who does little more than record events. This narrator provides large chunks of history, giving a long view of the war, so readers can see the Henrys' story in the larger context of the conflict. Occasionally, Wouk provides the history lessons through his characters' conversations, as when Alistair Tudsbury explains to Pug how England is closely tied to Germany as a result of Queen Victoria's children and grandchildren having ruled it during the late nineteenth and early twentieth century (*WW*, 50).

On numerous occasions, however, Wouk writes from the point of view of his characters, taking readers into the minds of one of the

Henrys or of Natalie or Aaron Jastrow, in a method similar to that described by Henry James in the preface to *The Ambassadors*. He employs first-person narration less frequently, but there are two important "documents" written in the first-person that play a key role in helping to explain the war's causes and consequences: Aaron Jastrow's diary, begun after his capture by the Nazis, and German General Armin von Roon's memoirs, a two-volume reminiscence of the war that Victor Henry translates after his retirement from the navy. This latter document is an important device, for through von Roon's memoirs Wouk is able to present the war from the Germans' point of view—as Wouk reconstructs it, that is. Von Roon, a fictional member of Hitler's general staff, writes his memoir while serving time in prison for his war crimes, and provides both a macrocosmic military analysis of the great battles of the war and a confidential portrait of the madman who dragged the world into the conflict. Von Roon's discussion of the grand strategy employed by the Allies and the Germans, his analysis of the German campaigns in Poland and Russia, and their strategy for neutralizing Britain, and Japanese activities in the Far East, gives Wouk's novels an epic quality. Von Roon serves at times as an alter ego for the author, allowing him to praise Admiral Raymond Spruance's leadership at the battle of Midway lavishly, or to castigate both the American and Japanese naval commanders at the battle of Leyte Gulf. No American patriot could speak as von Roon does of the "imbecility" of Admiral Bull Halsey (outmatched, von Roon says, only by the "greater imbecility" of the Japanese commander Kurita), or dismiss the engagement at Leyte Gulf as a "military folly on the vastest scale" (*WR*, 1044). By placing such judgments in the mouth of a fictional character, who is already partially discredited because he is speaking from the losing side, Wouk is able to absolve himself of direct responsibility for such criticism.

There is another reason for Wouk's creating his fictional German memoirist. At one point von Roon observes that "Americans are apathetic toward their military history" (*WR*, 438). Wouk strongly believes this to be the case, and that America is the weaker for such apathy. He wants his own novels to correct the problem by providing a history lesson in the guise of entertainment—a noble goal, dating back to classical authors such as Horace, who states in *Ars Poetica* that the function of great literature is to teach and to delight.

Furthermore, because von Roon is an educated military professional, it is easy for him to make direct comparisons that Wouk might otherwise have to handle obliquely: particularly comparisons between World War II and the Napoleonic Wars. Undoubtedly, Wouk wants his readers to connect the mad Austrian corporal who led the German people to ruin with that earlier corporal whose dreams of world empire placed the European continent in turmoil for two decades—and in the process gave Tolstoy a subject for what many consider the greatest of all novels, *War and Peace*. Throughout the text of both novels, Wouk alludes to Tolstoy's epic, which tells the story of a Russian family displaced by Napoleon's invasion of their homeland.[14] At one point, the intellectual Leslie Slote recalls that Tolstoy's "grand theme" in *War and Peace* is the transformation of Napoleon "in Pierre Bezukhov's mind from liberal deliverer of Europe to bloodthirsty invader of Russia" (*WR*, 600). Wouk wants his readers to judge Hitler in similarly harsh terms.

In addition to the many references, both veiled and direct, to Tolstoy's novel, Wouk includes numerous other comparisons to epic literature. For example, Alistair Tudsbury describes Victor Henry and his two sons as "three figures from the Iliad" (*WR*, 258). Von Roon accuses American Admiral Chester Nimitz of less-than-honorable behavior in ordering the attack on Admiral Yamamoto's plane in 1943 by saying that "Between Achilles and Hector, there might have been more honor than this sneak murder" (*WR*, 256). Through the voice of his omniscient narrator, Wouk compares the Japanese pilot who spotted the American carriers off Midway but failed to report them to his superiors to the asp that bit the empress Cleopatra, "small creature on whom the fortunes of an empire had briefly and sadly turned" (*WR*, 337). In praise of the American torpedo plane pilots who died en masse attacking the Japanese force at Midway, Wouk remarks that "the old sagas" would have included a list of their names so that they could achieve immortality through literature for their heroism: "Let this romance follow the tradition," he continues; then he provides a page of the names and hometowns of those who lost their lives in that heroic action (*WR*, 340 ff.).[15] Finally, using the voice of his omniscient historian, Wouk notes that in the battle of Leyte Gulf, highly advanced communications systems allowed the senior commanders in Hawaii and Washington to be like "Homeric gods, hovering overhead," or "like Napoleon on a hill at Austerlitz" (*WR*, 1028). Clearly, these comparisons reinforce the idea that behind Wouk's multiple plots, varied characters, shifting narrative voices, and combinations of macrocosmic historical overviews with dramatic creations of fictional dialogue between star-crossed lovers, lies a unifying purpose.

Themes of Valor and Remembrance

The grand theme of *The Winds of War* and *War and Remembrance* is expressed succinctly in the words of Victor Henry near the end of the second volume. Reflecting on the impact of the introduction of atomic warfare by the United States, Henry declares: "Either war is finished, or we are" (*WR*, 1055). The seriousness of Wouk's purpose in composing the story of the Henry family can be seen in his remarks to a *Publisher's Weekly* reviewer: "World War II . . . was an Everest of human experience . . . It started with a horse-drawn army moving into Poland and ended with the atomic bomb. Its outcome was crucial to the human race . . ."[16]

In these two novels Wouk is able to combine two lifelong interests in a single story: his love for the military, especially the navy, and his devotion to his Jewish heritage. Depicting the events of World War II gives him ample opportunity to examine both the navy and the Jews in a time of great crisis. As one might imagine, in Wouk's version both survive the struggle and distinguish themselves repeatedly in their life-and-death battles with the forces of darkness. Additionally, Wouk uses these novels as vehicles for preaching his own brand of pacifism, an unusual blend of liberal chanting for disarmament and universal renunciation of militarism, peppered with a consistently conservative call for heeding those who caution against believing too strongly that the world can be made safe for all people at all times.

Wouk's love for the navy has never been in question. He seems to rise to his highest level of artistic capability when writing about military operations; as Pearl Bell notes, "the most powerfully rendered episodes" in these works are often the "meticulously documented accounts of the great navy victories at Midway and Leyte Gulf." The "brilliantly evocative account of battle" gives readers the sense that the author has "mastered every maneuver" (Bell, 71). Further, "traditionalist support of the military career man which Wouk asserted in his earlier work," Richard Bolton notes, "becomes a pervasive theme in *The Winds of War*" (Bolton, 393). Insinuated in *The Caine Mutiny*, it becomes transparent in *The Winds of War* and *War and Remembrance*: Wouk has great admiration for the men who have chosen to pursue the military as a way of life, and though on occasion one of them might turn out to be like Philip Queeg, the majority are more like Victor Henry, "men of strong convictions, whose life and thought moves in a positive and strong tradition . . . men of good will who . . . devote their lives to industrialized armed force" (Bolton, 397).

According to Bolton, Wouk thinks that, though war is always a disaster, its effects can be ameliorated if the military professional is accepted and respected as a necessary element of society; unfortunately, democratic societies "have little stomach for the unpleasant facts that are a military professional's daily fare" (Bolton, 398). These "men of good will," as Bolton calls them, focus their professional goals on the constructive elements of a profession that is ironically bent on destruction; men like Pug Henry want to command a battleship because doing so gives them "the satisfaction of managing and ordering such a mechanism" (Bolton, 402). "In Wouk's view," Bolton continues, military professionals are "not warmongers or deliberate killers," but rather are "victims of war rather than promoters of it" (Bolton, 404).

Such views are not compatible with contemporary democratic sentiments, to be sure, where military professionals are castigated as warmongers or dismissed as careerists concerned only with personal glory. Wouk makes a strong case for the integrity of the profession throughout the novels. The question is raised early in *The Winds of War*, when Rhoda describes Pug to Palmer Kirby as "a patriot." Kirby asks shrewdly, "Is he a patriot, or is he a Navy career man? Those are two different things" (*WW*, 270). It recurs throughout the narrative, both in the inner thoughts of serving professionals such as Pug and Warren, and in the musings of outsiders such as Leslie Slote, who considers military men to be "grown-up boy scouts . . . banal narrow-minded conservatives to a man" (*WR*, 607). Wouk's own ideas are quite different. His professionals show themselves to be resourceful, dedicated to their cause, and genuinely concerned about the war's effects on both soldiers and civilians. Scattered throughout the narrative are vignettes that highlight the humanity of the officer corps, such as the exchange between Pug and Russian General Yevlenko when the latter takes his American counterpart for a tour of Leningrad after the famous siege. Making exceptionally good use of understatement, Wouk has the Russian remark that his mother had died in the siege. Pug's expression of sympathy includes the question, "Was she killed in the bombardment?", to which Yevlenko replies, "No. She starved" (*WR*, 689). The chapter ends on that somber note.

Through his hero, Wouk attacks the idea forcefully argued by Tolstoy in the epilogue to *War and Peace*, that grand strategy means nothing in battle; he agrees, though, that victory depends in great part on the "individual brave spirit in the field" (*WR*, 1053), and his accounts of the various battles are intended to show how both famous and forgotten fighters shape the course of wars. While he presents Admiral Raymond

Spruance as a hero, comparing his actions at Midway to those of Nelson at Trafalgar (*WR*, 350), he also makes it clear that many unknown men, like the torpedo pilots who sacrificed themselves to wreck the Japanese carriers, and ship commanders like Victor Henry who may not have even seen immediate action in the fray, all contributed to American success in the Pacific.

As he does in *The Caine Mutiny*, Wouk also examines the pressures of command, especially in battle. Through brief portraits of various men who rise to command small boats, major warships, or entire fleets, Wouk is able to show the stresses that such duty places on men, and the ways their responses to the pressures of leadership help determine the ultimate success of a fighting force. Victor Henry emerges as a model of the naval commander—and a counterpoint to Philip Queeg. Pug is technically competent, cool under pressure, willing to admit his mistakes, tough when he needs to be, but unwilling to take advantage of his position by usurping the rights and privileges of those who serve under him. He proves a hard taskmaster when he assumes command of the *Northampton* (*WR*, 175), but the additional training he orders pays off when his ship is thrust into battle. These characteristics are shared by other commanders, whose methods Wouk briefly sketches. Most notable among them is Carter Aster, Byron's skipper aboard USS *Moray*, a shrewd risk-taker who earns glory for his ship and for himself by pursuing his missions aggressively. Byron, too, proves to be a good commander who remains cool under the most punishing attacks by Japanese destroyers.

There are both historical and fictional commanders who, like Queeg, become the object of Wouk's scorn. Byron's first submarine commander, Branch Hoban, exhibits Queeg-like behavior when his boat first goes into combat, blaming faulty torpedoes for his failure to carry out his first mission, while leaving the zone of operations with over 20 unfired projectiles (*WR*, 117). There is one important difference between Hoban and his fictional predecessor, though; after he cracks under the pressure of a destroyer attack, Hoban has the presence of mind to turn over command to Carter Aster so the safety of his crew is not placed in further jeopardy.

Wouk finds a real-life Queeg in Admiral Husband E. Kimmel, the commander of naval forces at Pearl Harbor on 7 December 1941. Pug Henry has an opportunity to meet briefly with Kimmel shortly after the Japanese attack, and he finds the admiral blaming everyone but himself for the devastation brought upon his forces. The fault, he tells Pug, lies with the army for not giving him warning, or with President Roosevelt, for failing to give the Pacific theater enough attention (*WW*, 990). His quirky mannerisms during the interview with Captain Henry are reminiscent of Queeg rolling his little steel balls to relieve the stress of command and ward off the need to admit failure.

Kimmel is not the only senior leader Wouk castigates. He also criticizes Admiral Bull Halsey, a man generally considered a hero of the war in the Pacific. In contrast to Spruance, whom Wouk reveres as a commander bent on winning battles with the least risk to his forces, Halsey is painted as a blowhard who is willing to act almost irrationally in pursuit of personal glory. Speaking through General von Roon, Wouk accuses Halsey of almost losing the Battle of Leyte Gulf by chasing after the Japanese carriers in an effort to "outdo Spruance" (*WR*, 1048). Through von Roon, Wouk also berates General Douglas MacArthur for demanding that the Americans include Leyte in their plans for neutralizing Japan; the base on that Philippine island had no tactical or strategic value, von Roon remarks, but MacArthur's landing there was necessary for "his great Return" to the islands. Hence, the "world's most massive sea battle" was waged for a prize that was "trivial," or worse, "useless" from a military standpoint (*WR*, 1045).

Wouk's aim in presenting the American military forces in a heroic light is much the same as Homer's in the *Iliad*: he wants his readers to understand that when a nation is in crisis, it can be saved only by the strong leadership of its warrior class, supported by thousands of anonymous soldiers and sailors whose heroism is an essential part of any victory. Wouk also wants to make it clear that military professionals have a place in the political structure of the country—not necessarily as leaders on the political scene, but as valued advisors. "Wouk is not advocating," Richard Bolton concludes, "that the Victor Henrys move into political charge, but rather that their advice and example be more attended to, both substantively and morally" (Bolton, 399).

The ability to make use of his top military men as advisors in times of crisis made Franklin Roosevelt, in Wouk's opinion, a particularly effective leader for America in times of war. Unlike Hitler or Mussolini (or even Stalin, for that matter), Roosevelt was always careful to pick his chief military commanders from among those men who had the talent for command; once he had appointed them, he let them conduct the war in the manner they felt was necessary to ensure victory. Furthermore, Roosevelt did not relieve or berate commanders who were beaten in tough encounters, and, unlike Hitler, he did not relieve commanders willy-nilly. While other world leaders may have criticized Roosevelt for paying Britain and Russia to fight America's war, Wouk sees this as the President's special strength, and characteristic of the American way of war. Victor Henry summarizes the author's own assessment of his country's overriding attitude toward combat: unlike Europeans, Americans always aim to "lose as few lives as possible, yet win battles and wars" (*WR*, 444). Hence, the true American hero is a President who arranges for Lend-Lease, or the admiral who strikes hard at the decisive moment, then withdraws to save his meager forces to fight another day: in short, Roosevelt and Spruance.

Wouk's second great concern is for the horrible impact of the war on the Jewish people. The story of Natalie and Aaron Jastrow, a major thread running through both novels, is used to dramatize the horrors of the Nazis' treatment of Jews. Numerous episodes provide graphic examples of the seemingly insatiable German appetite for inflicting pain on the Jews. What would make a nation or a political party focus so much hatred on one group of people? The story of Natalie and Aaron allows Wouk to focus on "the German question," as Michael Mandelbaum aptly describes it. Wouk wants to answer the seemingly inexplicable question: "Why did the Germans do it?" (Mandelbaum, 520). But Wouk is not content to explain the Germans' inhumanity; he wants also to probe the disturbing facts surrounding the Allies' unwillingness to take crisis of European Jewry seriously, though sufficient evidence was available before the war and during its early stages that Hitler's aim for the Jews was genocide.

The meticulous accounts of German atrocities scattered throughout the novels, and especially in *War and Remembrance*, need little explication. On the matter of the Allies' reluctance to assist the Jews, Wouk is forced to tread lightly for fear of offending readers who may be unwilling to see themselves or their forebears as somehow sharing in the crime of the Holocaust. To drive his point home, Wouk carefully constructs a number of scenes in which non-Jewish characters express their feelings or perform actions that reveal their true attitudes toward the Jews.

The American State Department official Leslie Slote is Wouk's representative of American attitudes. Having grown up in a neighborhood and attended schools where Jews were excluded, he is uncomfortable at the thought of having too many direct dealings with them; though he has had a long affair with Natalie before she met Byron Henry, he has never seriously considered marrying her because it would hamstring him in his career. At one point he even admits to himself that her being Jewish was "a flaw about half as bad as being a Negro" (*WR*, 414).

Ironically, Slote is the man to whom Aaron's cousin Berel Jastrow, a Polish Jew from a village near Auschwitz, delivers incontrovertible evidence of the Holocaust. Slote is ultimately convinced that he must do something to let people in Washington, including the President, know what is really happening behind German lines. Predictably, though, officials at the State Department and even at the White House are unwilling to act upon the evidence, making a series of excuses to hide their fear that too many Americans would find the thought of fighting to liberate the Jews too distasteful. Eventually Slote gives up, realizing that the treatment of the Jews simply does not matter to most Americans, who are more interested in the details of great battles such as that at El Alamein in Africa (*WR*, 558).

Other Americans are also willing to look the other way when confronted with German highhandedness or atrocities. The Henrys are able to find a remarkably lavish house in Berlin, because its Jewish owners have been forced to give up their property (*WW*, 57–59). Kip Tolliver, the officer whom Pug replaces as naval attaché in Berlin, dismisses the Nazis' treatment of the Jews as "a passing phase" that is really none of the Americans' business (*WW*, 11). Wouk believes that such misguided assessments contributed to the Holocaust, as much as the overt actions of the Nazi *Einsatzgruppen* (Special Action Units) which rounded up the Jews and sent them to death camps. If America can be wrong once, it can be wrong again, Wouk seems to be saying. Through these novels, Wouk tries to make his readers understand the nature of people who would act as the Nazis did, and people who would permit such actions—notably, Americans who chose not to act in support of the Jews.

Hence, many scenes in *The Winds of War* and *War and Remembrance* examine the character of the Germans, and indict those who let the Germans have their way. Leslie Slote gives an intellectual explanation for the rise of Nazism, a natural outgrowth of a unique confluence of nineteenth-century Germanic philosophy imposed on a long tradition of isolation and tribal pride traceable to Roman times (*WW*, 257). In Aaron Jastrow's journal, kept during the historian's months in various concentration and death camps, Wouk offers an assessment that is both intellectual and visceral. The Germans, Jastrow writes, "are different"; "orders cut all ties between them and us" (*WR*, 622). That is why men who were ordinarily good, law-abiding citizens could turn into monsters upon assignment to the *Einsatzgruppen* (*WR*, 725–26). Jastrow's most damning indictment—and hence, the author's—is his description of Adolf Eichmann, the architect of Hitler's Jewish policy. Eichmann is not

a "brute," nor a "banal bureaucrat"; he is much more frightening than
that. He is the "dread figure" that has "precipitated two wars . . . He is
one of us, a civilized man of the West . . . he is *the German*" (*WR*,
842–43, Wouk's emphasis).[17]

Wouk stresses the cruel and insensitive nature of the Nazis by having
his German memoirist, General Armin von Roon, continually excuse the
behavior of the German high command and the whole nation, as having
been misled by Hitler. Von Roon describes the adverse impact that
Hitler's treatment of the Jews had on soldiers serving on the eastern
front (*WR*, 67), and he repeatedly explains how those who opposed
Hitler were powerless to take action against him. Wouk intends for this
special pleading to ring hollow—and it does.

The German national character is not the only cause for the
Holocaust, however. Wouk levels criticism at outsiders, especially
Americans, for their willingness to permit Hitler to operate unchecked
even before hostilities broke out in 1939. "*We* created Hitler," Natalie
tells Slote, because America did not join the League of Nations, and
because the country followed isolationist policies after World War I
(*WW*, 609). Beneath America's thin veneer of tolerance for minorities
lies the same anti-Semitism that exists in Germany, a point Aaron makes
clear to his niece with the ominous warning that, should the war turn
out badly for the United States, "a defeated America will be uglier than
Nazi Germany" (*WR*, 193–4).

Wouk extends his criticism to the Christian community in general,
becoming bitter at times with Christian hypocrisy; in the voice of a
Jewish freedom-fighter, Wouk asks how it is that, though Christians
worship a man who was himself Jewish, they "go right on murdering
Jews" (*WW*, 969). A member of the Jewish underground in Italy suggests to Byron Henry that Christianity must bear some responsibility for
Hitler, since no one in the Christian community has stepped forward to
champion the Jews (*WR*, 471). Even a non-Jew voices this line of criticism: Bill Fenton, a pilot who flies Leslie Slote across the Atlantic on one
of the diplomat's many trips between Washington and the war zone,
asks Slote the rhetorical question of whether Stalin is really any better
than Hitler. Fenton answers his own question, denouncing the Soviet
leader as "the same kind of murderer," tolerated by Americans because
"he's *our* murderer" (*WR*, 554).

Wouk's exposition of the plight of the Jews during the Holocaust is
not merely a political statement. The suffering of his people under the
Nazis serves as a metaphor for a larger philosophical issue that the nov-

elist raises at key points throughout his work: the irrational evil that exists in even the most civilized societies. Through the thoughts of Aaron Jastrow, Wouk examines the problem of "senseless evil" (*WR*, 874).[18] In his journal, Jastrow offers a philosophical explanation for the problem. Extremism, he writes, is a "universal tuberculosis" in modern society, sealed off in most nations when times are good, but breaking out as a virulent disease in times of "social disorder, depression, war or revolution" (*WR*, 670). Our fate is to endure this evil, a part of fallible human nature, and to trust God that all will turn out right in the end. Though never mentioned in either novel, the image of the great biblical figure of Job looms in the background. Wouk sees the Jewish race condemned to live the life of Job on earth, constantly buffeted and tossed about by winds of destruction, asked to remember that their God will protect them because, despite their suffering, they are indeed a chosen people who will survive every adversity.[19]

Suffering and evil may be ineradicable components of human nature, but Wouk is not so certain that war is the necessary response to evil actions. Aaron Jastrow's plea to his fellow Jews to reject violence, based on the lesson of God's sparing Isaac from Abraham's knife, can be taken as Wouk's own motto: "God wants our love, not the ashes of our children" (*WR*, 477). The technology of modern warfare makes it even more imperative that further confrontations between nations be avoided. This is the purpose of "remembrance": to keep alive in the minds of those who may not personally have fought or suffered the ravages of warfare, the horrors that conflict brings to the world. Only then can future wars be averted. Yet at the same time, Wouk exonerates America for its rather drastic step in ending World War II by resorting to atomic warfare. Comparing it to the devastation inflicted by the Nazis at Auschwitz, he notes that the purpose of the Germans' death camps was "insane useless killing"; the aim of the Oak Ridge project that produced the atomic bomb was "to stop the global war unleashed by Germany" (*WR*, 908). Clearly in Wouk's view, the end justifies the means. He is not condoning warfare, but he seems quite willing to excuse even the most horrific forms of destruction if they are used for the greater good.

Critical Reception

The publication of these two novels once again assured Wouk a place in the spotlight of American letters, and at the center of another critical controversy. Not since *Marjorie Morningstar* had he received the kind of national attention that *The Winds of War* and *War and Remembrance* brought him. Dozens of magazines and newspapers devoted hundreds of column inches to discussing Wouk's fictional portraits and his accounts of the great American naval victories in the Pacific. Scholars and journalists debated the accuracy of his depiction of the Holocaust. And people all over America bought and read both massive volumes.

Writing in 1975, even before the appearance of *War and Remembrance*, Richard Bolton observed that Wouk's story of the war had become "a kind of phenomenon," not only in the realm of popular culture but also in "shaping a generation's perception of itself and its era" (Bolton 389). In the decade after the novels' publication, a number of reviewers joined Bolton in their praise for Wouk's accomplishment. Writing about *The Winds of War*, the reviewer for *Choice* observed that there "seems little question that this is Wouk's greatest achievement and, so far, the most successful attempt to capture the character of pre- and post–Pearl Harbor America."[20] Scholar Mark Charney agreed, rating *The Winds of War* with *The Caine Mutiny* as Wouk's best novels; both, he believes, "achieve . . . literary and thematic merit" (Charney 388).

War and Remembrance received similar accolades. The reviewer for *Publisher's Weekly* noted that this "long-awaited sequel . . . lives up to the scope and dramatic power of its predecessor"; the fictional characters "are fully realized, gripping the reader's affection and sympathy," and although its "panoramic sweep sometimes disrupts the coherence," the novel manages to exert a "superbly manipulated tug at the heartstrings, and makes a powerful statement about the tragedy and futility of war."[21] "Wouk is at his best" in the novel, Mark Charney posited, "when he uses descriptive passages to serve as detailed, all-too-realistic reminders of the suffering war brings" (Charney, 388). The pace of the narrative and the suspense Wouk creates drew special praise from *Commentary* reviewer Pearl Bell, who is generally not sympathetic toward the novelist's efforts: "The most glaring deficiencies of style and characterization," Bell notes, "dwindle to irrelevance, and austere literary standards crumble before the lust to find out what happens next and how it will all turn out" (Bell, 70).

Esquire critic Geoffrey Norman went even farther. He admits that "there is plenty that is bad about *War and Remembrance*"—when it "tries to be a novel" in the way we normally expect novels to be, it is "awkward and sometimes silly." But, he goes on, Wouk's ability to "make order out of the chaos that was World War II" is a remarkable achievement. Though he knew that the novel would undoubtedly be condemned by some as "prosaic and overlong," Norman predicted nonetheless that it "will endure longer than a good many tight little literary novels." "This," he says, "is just," because "the very best writing about war, in fact, is probably the very best writing there is—Thucydides, Shakespeare, Stendhal, Tolstoy, Hemingway. And now Herman Wouk."[22] This is select company indeed.

Wouk's elevation to this literary pantheon would not go unchallenged. A sampling of comments from reviewers less enamored of the two novels illustrates well the weaknesses that mar Wouk's performance in both *The Winds of War* and *War and Remembrance*. Though *The Winds of War* fared better than its sequel, a review of available criticism shows that comments directed at one novel mirror those made about the other. Generally, hostile critics attack Wouk's use of history, his techniques of composition and, as one might expect, his commitment to conservative ideology.

Pearl Bell compares Wouk's technique of including a sizable amount of factual information in his fictional narrative to similar efforts by novelists Arthur Hailey, James Michener, Colleen McCullough, and James Clavell. Novels by these popular writers are often little more than "stuffed geese," and Wouk is the worst of the lot at cramming in the results of his "prodigious research," serving up "encyclopedia slabs of information" to fatten his thin fictional plotline (Bell, 70). James Wolcott dismissed *The Winds of War* with the damning observation that "for all its attention to costumes, decor, tactics, and weaponry," the novel "is to history what *Dynasty* is to high finance"; the war is merely a "tumultuous backdrop for a lot of stolen kisses and impassioned hugs" (Wolcott, 76–7). Even a sympathetic critic such as Mark Charney found himself forced to admit that *War and Remembrance* seems "weighed down with interruptions for exposition of history" (Charney 387). Wouk is a "workmanlike, even accomplished, novelist," Michael Mandelbaum wrote in 1979, "but he is hardly to be compared to Tolstoy" (Mandelbaum, 518).

Attacks on the books' literary merits are even more harsh. Paul Fussell, who has written a number of literary and sociological studies of American wars, describes the "whole two-volume work" as "a very good popular history of the Second World War and the Holocaust in the guise of a very bad novel."[23] Bell remarked that while it was impossible not to admire Wouk's research efforts or to deny "the dignity and decency" of his sense of "moral obligation" in telling his story, *War and Remembrance* "still cannot by any valid standard be judged a successfully realized work of literature" (Bell, 72). The fault, Bell continued, lies in Wouk's inability "to free his imagination from the stale and debilitating conventions of popular fiction" (Bell, 72). A similar objection was made to *The Winds of War* by P. S. Coyne, who argued in the *National Review* that had Wouk "limited himself to a novelistic study of the four great leaders of World War II," the novel "could have been an important step toward the revitalization of the American historical novel." Unfortunately, it is "heavy with creative writing techniques and plot demands," as a result of which the reader senses that World War II and Rhoda's adulterous behavior have "the same cosmic significance."[24] Pearl Bell attributes this unfortunate levelling of all issues to the lowest common denominator to Wouk's conscious effort to reach the widest possible readership: "Wouk makes no bones about the reader he aims to please," and therefore "an undemanding vividness and ease takes precedence at all times over any daunting complexities of thought, craft, or human behavior" (Bell, 70).

A significant number of reviewers took special exception to Wouk's characters. Paul Fussell dismissed Victory Henry as "not to be believed." He accused Wouk of creating characters and a plot that was "purely 1950s Metro-Goldwyn-Mayer" (Fussell, 32). A similar criticism was leveled at the author by Melvin Maddocks, who remarked that Wouk "thinks and feels and even writes as if he were still in the 1940s."[25] The "stick figures" of Wouk's war novels, said Fussell, are necessary to the author because "without typecasting everybody and everything Wouk would be lost in a world more complicated than he and his readers can tolerate" (Fussell, 32).

Maddocks carries these charges a step farther: "Wouk appears as reluctant to develop his ideas as his characters" (Maddocks, 16). Here we hear faint echoes of the attacks made by liberal critics for more than 40 years against the novelist: Wouk is unashamedly conservative in his political outlook, and overtly supportive of traditional American values. It is no wonder that Fussell, who in his own works is highly critical of the military establishment, considers *The Winds of War* and *War and Remembrance* "Wouk's retrograde middle-class allegory of success" (Fussell, 32).[26] Pearl Bell offered a note of warning that because Wouk "remains an unembarrassed believer in such 'discredited' forms of commitment as valor, gallantry, leadership, patriotism," reviewers will find his war novels "at best naive, at worst absurdly out of touch with the Catch-22 lunacy of all war" (Bell, 70).

Appearing as they did in 1971 and 1978 respectively, at the end of America's longest and most divisive conflict, neither novel could have been expected to fare well with critics with antiwar inclinations. Though he makes only veiled references to Vietnam in his novels, Wouk believed his works could help his readers understand why America had gotten involved there. "To find out," he told reporter Karen Howard, "you have to go back to World War II, the great modern historical watershed" (Howard, 54). Wouk himself acknowledged that "in writing a novel like *The Winds of War* I had to swim upstream against the current antihero vogue" (Bannon, 45). Certainly Karen McPherson's observation that "changes in the image of the military in fiction" generally correspond to "a more general change in social attitudes toward the military" is a truism hardly worthy of dispute (McPherson, 647). Therefore, one must be careful not to dismiss either novel as second- or third-rate simply because the criticism tends to be negative. Rather, the division between highbrow reviewers and purchasers at large gives credence to Richard Bolton's observation that the "leadership and direction" that heroes like Pug Henry provide for America "may not seem appealing to academics, but a poll of the customers of all drugstores where *The Winds of War* has appeared in paperback might yield quite different results" (Bolton, 405).

At the risk of digressing, I will cite an additional defense of Wouk's method and his accomplishments. Arnold Beichman defends the war novels against the host of critics who have castigated them by suggesting that Wouk has managed to capture the essence of war's horrors and its devastating effect on participants and noncombatants alike, without stooping to the level of graphic sex and violence found in other works within the genre. The novels, he says, have become best-sellers "without formulaic gobs of eroticism, perversion, hallucinating onanism, incest, lesbianism, necrophilia, and a generalized scatology. A unique achievement these days" (Beichman, 90). It is true that neither novel contains graphic descriptions of sex, and little direct description of senseless violence. Ironically, however, Beichman seems to ignore Wouk's "progress" in reporting graphic language: both *The Winds of War* and *War and Remembrance* are shot through with four-letter words, something Wouk avoided in earlier novels. Wouk seems to have developed a politician's sense about his use of language: he is willing to give the public exactly what it has come to accept from others, but no more.

Clearly the level of rhetoric runs high in both favorable and negative reviews of these novels. I believe Wouk's literary artistry warrants a more careful look to determine its merits. Certainly, some of the literary criticism, and criticism aimed at Wouk's handling of history, stems from a misunderstanding of genre. Richard Bolton notes that critics who have "castigated" these novels as *novels* have seemingly overlooked the author's classification of both his works as romances "whose purpose is to dramatize the author's ideas about his themes" (Bolton 340–41). According to Bolton, Wouk thinks World War II can teach us how to live even in "a more ramified and ambiguous world situation"—if we are willing to remember the past (Bolton, 407).

Perhaps there is something to Bolton's approach, but it makes light of Wouk's significant ability to render vivid descriptions of war scenes—something even many of his detractors find worthwhile in both novels. Any reader who wants evidence of the special literary strengths of either book need only turn to scenes in which Wouk describes one of the major engagements of the war. I would agree with Geoffrey Norman that "Nobody, not even Samuel Eliot Morison, has ever handled the Battle of Midway better" (Norman, 96). Wouk's description of Midway ranks with the best military writing, fiction or history. His ability to move confidently from panoramic view to specific action is particularly effective. Selectively cutting from the Japanese to the American sides, carefully constructing scenes in which Spruance and Nagumo maneuver their forces or in which the thousands of participants—including both Victor and Warren Henry—carry out the strategy of their commanders, Wouk gives his readers the sense of fog that surrounds naval battles, and the dependence of such engagements on the courage of the individual sailors and their commanders (*WR*, 333 ff.). Similarly, he handles the suffering of the Russians at the siege of Leningrad with special poignancy (*WR*, 690 ff.).

Wouk's use of multiple points of view adds special drama to the events he describes. One that stands out is his presentation of the Japanese attack on Pearl Harbor. Rather than focus on the pilots conducting the attack or on the American sailors caught by surprise on that fateful Sunday morning, he chooses instead to create the scene as it is viewed by Warren Henry's wife Janice, who leaves her Hawaiian bungalow early on the morning of 7 December 1941, to find some medicine for her sick infant. She witnesses the attack as she drives down the hill on which she lives toward Pearl Harbor, like some parody of an Olympian god viewing the slaughter on the plains of Troy. Wouk does not make such a comparison, however; he lets the action speak for itself. Detailing Janice's reaction—which includes a rather nasty altercation with a Japanese-American drugstore owner—seems a particularly apt illustration of the extent to which Americans were taken aback by the "effrontery" of their Asian adversaries. Janice's unspoken thoughts—how *dare* this happen to America!—serve as metaphor for her country's surprise and indignation.

In both *The Winds of War* and *War and Remembrance*, Wouk demonstrates that he can on occasion turn a phrase and capture a sweeping thought in a single sentence. Consider his description of the demise of the British empire, a long process finally brought to completion by World War II. "When an empire dies," Wouk writes, "it dies like a cloudy day, without a visible moment of sunset" (*WR*, 105). To allow his readers to imagine the disarray at Midway, when the Japanese ships sail to and fro while trying to avoid American air attack, he compares the wakes of their ships, crisscrossed and curled over each other, to "a child's finger painting white on blue" (*WR*, 343). Unfortunately, he sometimes overuses a good metaphor, as when he aptly describes service families as "tumbleweeds" (*WW*, 949)—then uses the same word twice more within three pages to characterize the Henry family, which has been separated by the vicissitudes of war.

One might best judge Wouk's technical performance in these novels as uneven. At his best in recounting history or describing military operations, the novelist seems to have significant trouble rendering romantic scenes, and some difficulty in depicting adult parent-child relationships. The primary weaknesses lie in creating dialogue and internal monologues for the various characters. Natalie's confession of love for Byron (*WW*, 311) comes off as stilted cliché. Janice's sudden declaration of love for Byron (coming after she is widowed, but whose motivation is questionable), includes "a wild kiss that dizzied, thrilled, and shot fire through" the younger Henry. To his surprised response, she promises "I won't eat you" (*WR*, 728). This language more closely resembles that of a cheap teenage romance rather than a novel where one might expect the author to delineate his character's responses more specifically. Janice's trite assurance seems particularly out-of-character for the daughter of a U.S. Senator—even an excited one.

The scenes between Victor Henry and Pamela are even more clumsily handled; cliché and emotionalism are the staples of Wouk's description of his hero's growing love for the young British woman. In one of their many partings (at least six occur over the years of their oft-interrupted courtship), the narrator reports that Henry finds it hard to express himself to Pam because "the sad, kind tones" of her voice were "choking his throat," and all his "rusty tongue" is able to mumble is "I'll never forget one minute of it" (*WW*, 529). The description of Pam's voice is vague at best, the dialogue placed in Henry's mouth is hardly more articulate than a schoolboy's. Most navy captains—even those dealing with a rather unusual situation—could probably do better. The passing years do not seem to help Pug, either. Much later, when the two meet in Iran, Pug thinks that maybe there is hope for him and Pam, since she has not yet married. It seems to him that their love "kept triumphing over time, over geography, over shattering deaths, over year-long separations" (*WR*, 851–52). At times, Wouk allows himself to get carried away beyond the limits of plausibility when writing about the effects of this new love in Pug Henry's life. When Pam finally tells Pug that she loves him, he immediately thinks that this might be his "God-granted chance to rebuild a ruined life" (*WR*, 266). Coming after over 1,000 pages detailing Henry's career and family successes—not a perfect life, by any means, but one with significant triumphs—such a reaction seems overblown. It would be easy to find similar dialogue and description in passages about Rhoda and Kirby, Byron and Natalie, Warren and Janice, or even Madeline and Simon Anderson, her navy beau. Are we to assume that these people are all shallow, or has the author simply not worked hard enough to render these scenes sufficiently specific to evoke the feelings of his characters, rather than insisting on them?

Such criticism need not overshadow the significant accomplishments of plotting, historical description, and suspense that are the special strengths of these novels. Nor does it necessarily negate the immediacy of Wouk's powerful portrait of an American family pulled apart by the war, forever changed by events that force them to take on roles few had anticipated. Despite the occasional lapses of style, the Henry family's tragedies and triumphs remain a powerful metaphor for middle-class America's involvement in the Second World War. This is not quite an epic, but it is certainly far from a simple third-rate popular potboiler.

Coming into American Homes: ABC's Mini-Series

In an interview given shortly after the appearance of *The Winds of War* in 1971, Wouk doubted that his novel would make a good movie, since "the scope is too great" (Howard, *Life*, 55). Certainly, this remark has to rank as one of most ironic in recent memory. Not until *War and Remembrance* was almost completed, however, was there serious consideration of bringing Wouk's version of World War II to the screen. In 1977, television and movie executive Barry Diller worked out a deal in which the American Broadcasting Company paid Wouk $1.5 million to help develop a television mini-series based on *The Winds of War*. In the years to follow, Wouk would work out a deal for *War and Remembrance* as well. The original contract allowed the author significant control over the project, including selection of both producer and director; he was also given a role in determining the program's sponsors. Wouk worked on the teleplay, and began a long-distance commute between Washington and a new abode in Palm Springs, California.[27]

The "story behind 'The Winds of War' production," *Publisher's Weekly* reported in 1982, "looms as large as the story of the novel itself." Its production costs—$40 million—made it the most expensive mini-series to date, and its 18-hour run ranked it as the second-longest mini-series yet produced.[28]

As had happened with the movie production of *The Caine Mutiny, The Winds of War* attracted a cast of stars whose name recognition did much to boost ratings. Longtime Hollywood tough guy Robert Mitchum landed the role of Victor Henry. Polly Bergen was cast as Rhoda. Jan Michael Vincent played the irascible Byron Henry, Ali McGraw the invincible Natalie Jastrow, John Houseman her uncle Aaron. Relative newcomer Victoria Tennant won the enviable part as Pamela Tudsbury. Virtually every other role of any significance was taken by an actor or actress of some stature (Peter Graves had the not-so-impossible mission of playing Palmer Kirby, for instance, and Topol created the character of Berel Jastrow—without fiddle); many viewers spent considerable time waiting for the next star to make a cameo appearance.[29]

Though at least one initial review found it "dull and slow-moving" (*Variety*, 66), the show netted a "hefty 53 share of the audience" in television ratings—placing it somewhere near the best-watched sporting events in the country.[30] ABC reported that the show was the "most watched program in television history"; the network's research bureau estimated that 140 million people watched "some segment" of the program (*Time*, 63). Reviews were mixed—as they usually are for any major popular television production. The major criticisms focused on Mitchum's performance, which most found strained. As *Variety*'s reviewer noted, "Mitchum remained a disappointment. He's just not right for the part" (*Variety*, 66). That assessment seems most appropriate, since in 1980 Mitchum was already a decade or more older than the fictional Victor Henry; from the opening scene, he looked much more like a retired admiral than an up-and-coming commander. The problem was exacerbated when the sequel was filmed several years later, as Mitchum appeared even older, despite attempts to hide his age through creative make-up.

It would have been too much to expect that, when Wouk and his partners from the television industry were ready to film *War and Remembrance*, every actor who had appeared in *The Winds of War* would return to their roles. Fortunately, Mitchum, Bergen, Tennant, and many others did come back. Again, one of life's more amusing ironies surfaced in casting for roles in *War and Remembrance*. Writing about *The Winds of War* in 1983, reviewer John Wolcott commented sardonically that he was "very suspicious of any mini-series that doesn't feature Jane Seymour."[31] Perhaps someone in Hollywood or New York took that remark to heart, for Seymour was hired to replace Ali McGraw as Natalie Jastrow in the sequel. Unlike its predecessor, however, the *War and Remembrance* mini-series did not fare well in the ratings. Since the sequel was even longer than the original series, ABC decided to divide the showings across the television season. The initial segments were shown in the fall of 1988, and ABC planned to air the second half during the February ratings sweeps. Response to the first week's showings in the fall was so lackluster, however, that the network delayed showing the second half until it had a slow week and needed a "fill."

As one might expect, neither televised version does complete justice to Wouk's novels. Perhaps Wouk was right to suggest that their scope was too great. Many viewers were confused by the story line, especially in *The Winds of War*. To rectify this problem, the writers (presumably with Wouk among them), chose to limit the scope of the sequel severely, so that if one watches the television series without reading the book, one might believe that *War and Remembrance* is primarily the story of Natalie Jastrow's efforts to escape from the Nazis. Almost no attention is paid to the great naval battles that are the heart of Wouk's novel. After *The Winds of War* had completed its run on television, Wouk told a *Time* reviewer that he thought the televised version was as faithful to his novel as possible, though he admitted that no more than 15 to 20 percent of his published work made it to the screen: "Film always simplifies," he remarked, "and this is a simpler version of my story, my people, and the history."[32] I think Wouk is only partially correct. The major strength of his novels is their complex plot and panoramic sweep of the world at war. Neither television production captures the sense of breadth that one feels in reading the novels. It would be a shame if these celluloid redactions were to be viewed as appropriate substitutes for the novels from which they were drawn.

Chapter Six

"Shooting for the Family Trade"

Inside, Outside: A Literary Paradigm

Summarizing an author's critical concerns is not always easy, but fortunately in Wouk's case, the novelist has simplified the task. In 1985, he published *Inside, Outside*, a highly autobiographical novel that depicts the boyhood adventures of a man who has risen to prominence in American society. I believe the work may be used as a paradigm in explaining Wouk's position as a conservative, popular Jewish novelist in America.[1] The hero, Israel David Goodkind, is a highly successful lawyer. In the novel's present, he has put aside his liberal prejudices to accept an appointment as cultural adviser to Richard Nixon. The year is 1973; the Watergate investigations are taking a large toll on the president and his closest confidants, while in the Middle East tensions between Israel and its Arab neighbors are again approaching the breaking point. As the crisis in the Middle East reaches a crescendo, he is called upon to serve as a special envoy for his country in negotiations with Israeli Prime Minister Golda Meir; his efforts are instrumental in negotiating United States aid for the Jewish state in the 1973 Arab-Israeli war.

Goodkind's adventures in shuttle diplomacy constitute only a small portion of the novel. He is largely unoccupied for much of his time at the White House, so he spends his spare hours writing an account of his early life as a Jew growing up in New York City. Consistently narrated in first-person, the novel shifts between the political crisis of 1973 and events some four or five decades earlier, during Goodkind's boyhood and early adult life. Readers familiar with the details of Wouk's life will recognize the novel's highly autobiographical nature. The intellectually gifted second child (Wouk was third in his family) of Russian immigrant parents (as Wouk's were), Goodkind lives a life completely dominated by religious practices and customs. Meanwhile, his father, the owner of a laundry business (like Wouk's own father), tries to make a good life for his wife and children and for others in his *mishpohka*, or extended family. David attends Columbia University, forsakes law school to take a job as a gag writer, and eventually falls in love with a non-Jewish woman. With the exception of the last incident, which is not documented in any available source about Wouk, the events in Goodkind's life are remarkably like those of his creator.

Further dramatic interest in the novel comes from the continual contrast between the "inside" of Orthodox Jewish life and the demands of the "outside" world, specifically American society, with the intense pressure for assimilation that it places on minority ethnic and religious groups. At home, the hero is called Israel; outside, in school and in the world of work, he is David. Inside, family values and traditional attitudes toward sex and marriage dominate; outside, there is a strong call to adopt the lax moral code of twentieth-century America. The novel also offers insight into the experience of prejudice, as David is derided by insensitive Christian children near his neighborhood who call him a "Christ-killer" and taunt him with chants of "Izzy" (a diminutive of his given name that in the 1920s carried overtones of mockery and disdain).

Like his hero, Wouk has been a victim as well as a victor. Despite his commercial success, he has never been fully accepted by literary society in America. He has made few public appearances, participated in few public causes, and been either overlooked or intentionally ignored by critics who have been most influential in shaping literary tastes during the second half of the century. Like the fictional Goodkind, Wouk has wanted to have things both ways. Though he has often presented politically and morally liberal point of view sympathetically, he has always come back to his basic conservative values; they are at the heart of his personal philosophy, grounded in Orthodox religion.

Inside, Outside offers Wouk a forum for blasting Jewish novelists who have turned away from their heritage, or worse, used it as an object of scorn in an attempt to reach a wide readership. Goodkind's friend and client, Peter Quat, has achieved immense popularity by writing salacious tales full of deviant sex. Presumably, Quat is a thinly disguised portrait of Philip Roth, author of the comic novel *Portnoy's Complaint* (1968) and other works featuring Jewish characters and filled with the trappings of psychological fiction.

Wouk will have no truck with such fellows, even if it costs him some readers. Speaking directly to readers, David Goodkind says he knows his reminiscences will never match the sales of his friend Peter Quat's books, because "I'm shooting for the family trade."[2] Indeed, that telling statement explains as much about Wouk's method as it does about his subject matter, since it places him squarely in the camp of popular novelists who shun shock techniques in order to avoid offending their readers. This is not necessarily the place to occupy if one also aims to please academic and "highbrow" literary critics in the twentieth century.

It is also important to realize that, as a popular novelist, Wouk is fighting a strong trend against his work's acceptance as art. As the distinguished literary historian Arnold Kettle observed in 1967, "The most striking and in some respects the most alarming feature in the development of the novel in the twentieth century has been the ever-increasing separation between the 'good' and the 'popular' . . . both the middlebrow best-seller and the mass-produced reading material of the majority of the people is despised and almost unread by the intellectuals."[3] Wouk has intentionally separated himself from liberal novelists and those who have adopted the techniques of modern psychology for exploring characters and incidents in their fiction. Also, he has distinguished himself from many of his contemporaries by refusing to celebrate modernist values or adopt modernist techniques of characterization. In one of his few public appearances at a literary event, a Book-and-Authors luncheon in 1972, Wouk spoke about "the antihero as the de rigueur central figure of contemporary literature." Citing the "four great archetypes" of modern fiction—"Leopold Bloom, the narrator in *Remembrance of Things Past*, Joseph K. in Kafka's *The Trial*, and the anonymous narrator in Dostoyevsky's *Notes from Underground*—Wouk concludes that the figure who dominates modern literature, often an acute observer of contemporary life, is essentially impotent."[4] Wouk's heroes are all doers, not observers. Realizing that he is "swim[ming] upstream" against the trend toward sensitivity and inaction in literary heroes, Wouk consciously creates characters who are (at least in his view) full of life and prone to action; if they are less introspective than the contemporary reader might expect, this lack is compensated by their efforts to make the world a better place for themselves and others.[5] Another telling remark from *Inside, Outside* offers insight into the kind of hero Wouk really admires. To illustrate the nature of comedy, the gagman who hires Goodkind makes the following point about Shakespeare's greatest comic creation, Falstaff: "We love him, because we recognize ourselves in him. We love life as he does. We only wish we had the honesty to live it as he does . . . He is *us*. And it hurts so much to see ourselves in that bulging fun house mirror, distorted and yet our true secret selves, that we laugh so as not to cry" (*Inside*, 379). Certainly not all of Wouk's characters are Falstaffs; but the best of them love life dearly, and eventually learn to accept their fate cheerfully. In the process, they learn to laugh at themselves, if they don't end up dying a bitter, even tragic death. This example also gives us a clue to the authors Wouk wishes to emulate. He is not interested in competing with James Joyce or Philip Roth; he wants to be considered a descendant of the creators of Falstaff, Don Quixote, Tom Jones, and David Copperfield. At the moment, the jury is still deciding how well he has measured up, but in a literary world where optimism and action on behalf of society are given little credence, he is having a hard time getting a fair hearing.

Wouk's Weaknesses and Strengths

If one can move beyond the political rhetoric that has characterized so much discussion of Wouk's novels to focus on literary technique, it may be possible to judge Wouk's merits as an author. I would suggest that, though certain weaknesses run through all his fiction, strengths emerge that mark him as substantially better than the average popular writer, whose aim is only to provide titillation, excitement, or escapism for readers.

I will first consider the weaknesses. Wouk has always had difficulty creating realistic romantic scenes. Those in *Aurora Dawn* can be excused because the novel is a satire; one expects laughable scenes of stilted language and professions of love, similar to scenes in classic fiction such as Fielding's *Joseph Andrews*, a conscious model for Wouk's story. When such scenes are central to the work, however, as in *Marjorie Morningstar* or *Youngblood Hawke*, the author's inability to rise above the level of cliché is a serious flaw. What seemed sophomoric in *The Caine Mutiny* remains so in both *The Winds of War* and *War and Remembrance*, though Wouk had almost two decades to work out the problems of dialogue and description that critics pointed to in his earlier book. For example, Natalie tells Byron that her love for him makes her feel "weird" and "disembodied," and surmises that she may simply be "drunk on kisses"; Byron replies that what she feels is "damned real," that "reality just seems to be starting" (*WW*, 398). Similarly, when Pug has difficulty feeling any sexual passion for Rhoda when he returns to Washington after his ship is sunk in the Battle of Tassafaronga, he thinks that he ought to "throw off his bridge coat" and "seize her" (*WR*, 570). These phrases and sentiments are common in cheap paperback romances; one hopes for something better from a novelist who wishes readers to take his work seriously.

Similarly, Wouk's descriptions of women tend to be vague. Examples from his war novels may serve to illustrate the point. Both are descriptions of Janice Lacouture, the socialite daughter of a Florida senator whom Warren Henry eventually marries. Victor Henry's first impression of his future daughter-in-law is as "another, early Rhoda, swathed in cloudy pink, all composed of sweet scent, sexual allure, and girlish grace" (*WW*, 190). Later, at a lawn party, Janice cuts this figure as she moves among the crowd: "The white satin, clinging to flanks and breasts like creamy skin, rose demurely to cover her throat. She moved in a cloud of white lace." For Wouk, it all adds up to a "blend of white chastity and crude fleshy allure" (*WW*, 413). The combination of abstraction and cliché does little to create a specific image of the senator's daughter.

In sum, when handling romance, Wouk seems to believe that simply saying something will make it real for his readers; he fails to make his lovers come alive *as* lovers, leaving them to wallow in tired phrases and trite thoughts.

It also seems that Wouk could edit his own work more carefully. At times he slips into easy or extreme comparisons rather than striving to find a metaphor that is both fresh and appropriate. Again, I cite examples from the later war novels, because one would expect Wouk to have reached his peak as a novelist in them. Yet in describing Pug's naïveté regarding his wife's extramarital affairs, he writes that his hero could have no more imagined his wife's infidelity than he could have "suspected his wife of cannibalism" (*WW*, 760–61). These lapses into banality are not restricted to descriptions of matters of love. When Victor Henry, armed with an invitation from Churchill to participate in the British bombing raid over Berlin in 1940, finally arrives at the airfield and sees the cloth-covered plane in which he will fly, he feels "as compelled to enter" the aircraft as "a murderer is to climb a gallows to be hanged" (*WW*, 507). Byron Henry thinks the possibility of a Russian attack on Finland "as remote as a Chinese earthquake" (*WW*, 302), and when he gets a letter from his sister he considers the event as rare as "a total eclipse of the sun" (*WR*, 1101).

Virtually every one of Wouk's novels has been criticized for faulty or stereotypical characterization. In the case of *The Caine Mutiny* or *Marjorie Morningstar*, Wouk has been accused of wanting to have things both ways, creating characters who act one way for most of the novel, but who undergo a reversal that seems to redeem them in the eyes of their creator if not in the reader's judgment. Flaws in characterization are most acute in *Youngblood Hawke* and *Don't Stop the Carnival*, but charges have been leveled against characters in Wouk's better novels.

A look at *Inside, Outside* illustrates quite well what I believe often happens when critics approach a Wouk novel. Members of the Jewish community in that novel may appear to hardcore intellectuals as simply stereotypes: the Jewish mother who dotes on her gifted children; the Jewish father concerned with making money; aunts, uncles, cousins, and siblings sponging on the entrepreneurial relative; elderly grandparents berating the young for not being more attentive to their seniors and forever prodding them to study the Talmud and follow the laws of their religion. However, a sympathetic reader may discover that Wouk's portrait of the Jewish community in *Inside, Outside* makes its members lively, lovable, and quite believable as individuals. They can make the reader laugh or cry; their faults are as real as their strong points. They are, like members of any ethnic group, simply struggling to preserve their identity and make their way in an increasingly complex modern world.

The same may be said of many of the characters in the best of Wouk's novels. Perhaps because his works are so long, readers find themselves investing emotionally in Wouk's characters, and some faults of characterization are lost on those who consider the men of the *Caine*, the Morgensterns, and the Henrys as fellow travellers on life's rugged path. While Wouk's skill may not be equivalent to Dostoyevsky's or Henry James's ability to detail the innermost thoughts and feelings of complex characters, there is certainly some merit to his ability to gain and sustain readers' interest in the characters who people his best fiction.

To this one may add Wouk's ability on occasion to coin a particularly apt phrase or discover a vivid metaphor to describe a character or incident. Some of these have been cited in previous chapters, but a few additional examples may help support this judgment. In *Inside, Outside*, Wouk compares the notoriety of appearing in the news to "breath on a windowpane" (*Inside*, 6–7). In the same novel he observes that "childhood is a sequence of . . . traps, basic training in the dreary facts of life" (*Inside*, 58). In *War and Remembrance*, he describes the sight of the Japanese carriers drifting listlessly at sea after being destroyed by the American air attacks as "slaughtered bulls, dumped outside the bullring" (*WR*, 362). An author who can see the world so acutely, and capture it in words that bring it alive for readers, is certainly worthy of some critical attention.

Observations for Further Studies

The foregoing study is only preliminary. Many topics necessarily receive only brief mention, while others go unacknowledged, in an effort to provide an overview of a writer and his works. Before closing, it may be useful to point out three fruitful areas for further study of Wouk's novels and nonfiction.

First, unlike many popular novelists, Wouk fills his works with literary allusions. The dense texture of his stories is achieved through the interplay of Wouk's text with these references to the works of literary predecessors. A more comprehensive understanding of several of the novels, especially *The Caine Mutiny, Marjorie Morningstar, The Winds of War*, and *War and Remembrance*, may emerge from a careful look at Wouk's use of allusion. Other borrowings, such as parallels in structure or character development, may also bring to light new dimensions of Wouk's oeuvre.

Wouk is also an intensely personal novelist. More than many writers, he uses events from his own life in his fiction. Unfortunately, much information about his life is simply unavailable. Wouk has written no autobiography, no standard biography has been authorized, and no letters or unpublished documents are accessible to those wishing to conduct biographical studies of the author and his works.[6] As more information about Wouk's life and his methods of composition becomes available, scholars will be able to determine the extent to which the author has transformed life into art. Although he has not led the kind of life that makes for a blockbuster literary biography—he is no Hemingway—a scholarly "life of the author" will be a major contribution to Wouk studies. A useful offshoot of such a study would be an analysis of Wouk's relation to the community of Jewish-American writers, especially since he seems to be out of step with fellow successful Jewish writers.

Finally, several of the novels deserve more lengthy critical analysis. *Marjorie Morningstar* could be the subject of an examination of the Jewish novel's place in American literature. More study of *The Caine Mutiny, The Winds of War*, and *War and Remembarnce* is certainly needed. When it once again becomes fashionable to discuss the literature of warfare and command in battle, these works will make excellent subjects for analysis.

I must end on a cautionary note. Wouk is a passionate novelist, and he evokes strong passions in his readers. Not all of them respond positively to his brand of storytelling. Many may react as Tennyson did to Carlyle's *Frederick the Great*: midway through the book, his revulsion for Carlyle's reactionary brand of conservatism and unabashed hero-worship for the creator of the Prussian state reached a crescendo, and Tennyson flung the book into a corner in disgust. Some readers of Wouk have reacted (at least metaphorically) in the same fashion. If Wouk is to be given his due, critics must put aside their personal prejudices—something that is always difficult to do. It may be that, until the political pendulum swings back again, Wouk will have to wait for a final assessment of his place in American letters.

Notes and References

Preface

    1. Stanley Edgar Hyman, *Standards: A Chronicle of Books of Our Time* (New York: Horizon Press, 1966), 71.
    2. Cf. Arnold Beichman, *Herman Wouk: The Novelist as Social Historian* (New Brunswick, N.J.: Transaction Books, 1984), 77–78.
    3. Jeanne Braham, review of *Herman Wouk: The Novelist as Social Historian*, by Arnold Beichman, *Modern Fiction Studies* 31 (Winter 1985): 743.

Chapter One

    1. "The Wouk Mutiny," *Time*, 5 September 1955, 48; hereafter cited as "The Wouk Mutiny."
    2. *New York Post*, 17 January 1956, 39.
    3. Ibid.
    4. *This Is My God* (New York: Doubleday, 1959), 157; hereafter cited in text as *TIMG*. Wouk's notebooks, nonfiction writings and interviews are filled with loving references to his grandfather. When Rabbi Levine died in 1957, he willed Herman his set of the Vilna Talmud, perhaps his most prized possession.
    5. Arnold Beichman, *Herman Wouk: The Novelist as Social Historian* (New Brunswick, N.J.: Transaction Books, 1984), 9; hereafter cited in text.
    6. Details of Wouk's work as a radio gag writer can be found in Beichman, 9–19, and in William S. Hudson, "Herman Wouk: A Biographical and Critical Study," (Ph.D. diss., George Peabody College, 1969), Chapter III; hereafter cited in the text as "Hudson." Wouk provides a bittersweet fictional account of these years in his highly autobiographical novel *Inside, Outside* (Boston: Little, Brown, 1985).
    7. Henry Morgan was known as the "bad boy of radio." He began his career as an announcer in 1931, then hosted a series of shows from 1940 to 1950. He was noted for lambasting sponsors and station executives (including those of his own shows and network). A short account of his career is provided in John Dunning, *Tune In Yesterday: The Ultimate Encyclopedia of Old-Time Radio* (Englewood Cliffs, N.J.: Prentice-Hall, 1976), 273–75.
    8. Arnold Beichman observes that Wouk's 1947 article, "Make It with Kissing" (*'47: The Magazine of the Year* [November 1947], 14–21) provides a "serious examination . . . of American popular culture during what was the pretelevision age." In it, the novelist signals his "interest in how to achieve a degree of popular acceptance without compromising serious artistic standards"

(Beichman, 12–13). The struggle to retain popularity while striving to produce serious art has been at the center of Wouk's literary life since his first novel, *Aurora Dawn*.

9. Wouk did not end his association with the navy when the war ended and he received his discharge. He remained in the Navy Reserve for several years, and went to sea on occasion; in 1949, he spent time aboard USS *Saipan*, an aircraft carrier. In 1967, long after he had given up his reserve duty, he finagled a ride aboard the submarine USS *Sirago*.

10. *Book World*, 26 December 1971, 14.

11. Additional details regarding Wouk's success in landing a publisher for his first attempt at fiction are provided in Beichman, 16, and in Hudson, 110.

12. Introduction to *Self-Portrait of a Hero: The Letters of Jonathan Netanyahu* (New York: Random House, 1980), vi. Wouk's two other sons have grown to manhood: Nathaniel graduated from Princeton and took up a career as a writer; Joseph, a Columbia Law School graduate, emigrated to Israel to work with the Department of Justice there.

13. Cf. *TIMG*, 222, for Wouk's firsthand account of his first visit to Israel.

14. In an interview with *Time* magazine in 1954, Wouk observed of his work habits that he "reported to my boss, the desk, five or six days a week, at least six hours a day." He told the *Time* reporter of his preference for writing his first draft in longhand on yellow pads ("The Wouk Mutiny," 48).

15. For many years, Wouk appeared reticent—even squeamish—about including graphic sexuality in his works. He seems to have been uncomfortable with open discussion of such matters, perhaps masking his discomfort by dismissing the importance of graphic sexuality to a writer's success. The huge commercial success of his novels suggests that there was some truth to his belief that one did not have to be explicit about sex to sell books. It is hard to agree, though, with his observation that clinical examinations of sexual behavior such as the celebrated Kinsey Report had made sex "uninteresting" for the American public (cf. *TIMG*, 129).

16. *Book World*, 26 December 1971, 14.

17. Cf. *The Caine Mutiny* (New York: Doubleday, 1951), v. The limits of acceptability have expanded in the 30 years since Wouk wrote *The Caine Mutiny*, and he has slowly relaxed his own strictures regarding both language and incident. In both volumes of *War and Remembrance*, he includes words and expressions that he would have found offensive and smutty two decades earlier. Even more surprisingly, perhaps, in *Inside, Outside* he describes—in graphic detail—his hero's masturbation.

18. *New York Post*, 17 January 1956, 39.

19. The best source for understanding Wouk's attachment to Orthodoxy is *This Is My God*, which he wrote to explain his religion to non-Jews. Though Jewish scholars found it partially reductive and misleading, the

work remains a superb document of "confession" literature. In it, Wouk explains his reasons for returning to Orthodoxy (cf. 228–30, 294). Ironically, the work is reminiscent of Ernest Hemingway's *Death in the Afternoon* (New York: Scribner's, 1932). In both, one finds a primer of the author's philosophy of life and an explanation of the value system that underlies each's fiction.

20. Cf. *New York Post*, 17 January 1956, 39.

21. Ibid.

22. Other Edman titles include *Adam, the Baby, and the Man from Mars* (Boston: Houghton, Mifflin, 1929; New York: Books for Libraries Press, 1968); *The Contemporary and His Soul* (New York: J. Cape & H. Smith, 1931; New York: Kennikat Press, 1967); and *Four Ways of Philosophy* (New York: Henry Holt, 1937). Further references to these titles are cited in the text.

23. Charles Frankel, "Introduction" to Irwin Edman, *The Uses of Philosophy* (New York: Greenwood, 1968), 2; hereafter cited in text.

24. Wouk's opinions about the modern novel are presented succinctly in his article "You, Me and the Novel," *Saturday Review*, 29 June 1974, 8–13.

25. Edman 1929, 133–34. Edman does not totally dismiss the efforts of legitimate artists to experiment with new forms. In "Patterns for the Free," he notes that a few writers seek new forms because they find the old ones "inadequate to express those miscellanies of life hitherto inadmissible to the genteel tradition" (*Adam, the Baby, and the Man from Mars*, 147). Fifty years later Wouk echoes the same sentiments in a 1971 interview with a *Life* magazine reporter. Jane Howard, "Herman Wouk Surfaces Again," *Life* 71 (26 November 1971), 53–54; hereafter cited in the text.

26. Warren French suggested to me that the work to which Edman refers is Warwick Deeping's *Sorrel and Son*, a 1925 novel that shares certain affinities with Fitzgerald's *Great Gatsby*. For a discussion of this work, see Warren French, "(George) Warwick Deeping," *Twentieth-Century Romance & Historical Writers*, 2d ed. (Chicago: St. James Press, 1990), 172–73.

Chapter Two

1. Cf. Percy Atkinson, "Advertising Lightly Lampooned," *Saturday Review of Literature* 30 (19 April 1947), hereafter cited in the text; and Arnold Beichman, *Herman Wouk: The Novelist as Social Historian* (New Brunswick, N.J.: Transaction Books, 1984), 21; hereafter cited in the text.

2. Wouk relates the story of the novel's composition in the preface to the first edition, paying special attention to chronology in order to dispel rumors that he had "borrowed" from Frederic Wakeman's novel *The Hucksters*, which has a very similar subject and which was released before *Aurora Dawn*.

3. Cf. Luther F. Sies, "Tally Ho, Mr. Allen," *Journal of Popular Culture* 13:2 (Fall 1979), 165–66.

4. Diana Trilling, "Fiction in Review," *Nation* 164 (24 May 1947), 636; hereafter cited in text. Warren French has suggested that Irwin Edman,

Wouk's mentor, may have used his influence to get a critic of Diana Trilling's stature to review Wouk's first novel; Diana and Lionel Trilling were both members of the Columbia College circle which included Professor Edman.

5. In the Preface to the Pocket Books edition of 1983, Wouk indicates that in writing the book he adopted a "mask" that is "a caricature of Henry Fielding" (cf. *Aurora Dawn* [New York: Pocket Books, 1983], 6). These and subsequent citations are from this edition. Though some of Wouk's earlier novels are no longer in print in hardcover editions, after the success of *War and Remembrance* and the release of *The Winds of War* as a television mini-series, all of the novels were reissued in cheap paperback editions.

6. *Aurora Dawn*, 6.

7. Spencer Klaw, "A Delightfully Fresh and Funny Satire," *New York Herald Tribune*, 20 April 1947, p. 3, (hereafter cited in the text); Diana Trilling, "*Aurora Dawn*," *Kirkus Reviews* 15 (1 January 1947), 13; Trilling, *Nation*, 636.

8. Mark J. Charney, "Herman Wouk," *DLB Yearbook* (New York: Garland Press, 1982), 384; hereafter cited in the text.

9. "Herman Wouk," *The Booklist and Subscription Books Bulletin* 43 (1 May 1947), 273; Trilling, *Nation*, 636.

10. Klaw, 3; Atkinson's remarks are quoted in Charney, 384; "*Aurora Dawn*," *New York Times Book Review*, 20 April 1947, 5.

11. Details of Wouk's involvement in *Slattery's Hurricane* are related by Paul Nathan in "Books into Films," *Publisher's Weekly* 153 (14 February 1948), 996.

12. Thomas Sugrue, "Don Quixote from the Bronx," *New York Herald Tribune Weekly Book Review*, 29 August 1948, 4; hereafter cited in text.

13. *Kirkus Reviews* 16 (15 June 1948), 291.

14. W. Tasker Witham remarks that *City Boy* is one of the few twentieth-century novels to emphasize the masculine side of puppy love (*The Adolescent in the American Novel* [New York: Frederick Ungar, 1964], 32).

15. Allen Guttmann, *The Jewish Writer in America: Assimilation and the Crisis of Identity* (New York: Oxford University Press, 1971), 120; Richard B. Gehman, "Bronx Penrod," *The Saturday Review of Literature* 31 (21 August 1948), 10; hereafter cited in the text.

16. Marc Brandel, "Boy Meets Girl," *New York Times*, 29 August 1948, 10.

17. For a sampling of criticism, see Harold Clurman, review of *The Traitor, New Republic* 120 (18 April 1949), 30–31; "*The Traitor*," *Catholic World* 169 (1 May 1949), 145; "*The Traitor*," *Theater Arts* 33 (June 1949), 13; and Brooks Atkinson, "The Traitor," *New York Times Theater Review* 30 (1 April 1949), 2.

18. "Return of a Native," *Newsweek* 33 (11 April 1949), 79–80.

19. John Mason Brown, "New Plays in Manhattan," *Time* 53 (11 April 1949), 87.

20. Wouk to Cleveland Amory, quoted by Amory in "Trade Winds," *Saturday Review* 55 (12 February 1972), 8.

21. Cf. *"The Traitor," Catholic World*, 145, and Frederick I. Carpenter, "Herman Wouk," *College English* 17 (1956), 212.

Chapter Three

1. Cf. *This Is My God* (Garden City: Doubleday, 1959), 32–33, for Wouk's testimonial to the navy. Not only did Wouk continue to serve in the Naval Reserve for several years after World War II, he remained a friend of the navy even after he hung up his uniform for good. Though he generally avoids public appearances, in March 1972 he addressed the brigade of midshipmen at the Naval Academy as part of the Academy's prestigious Forrestal Lecture series. And despite the tight control he and his literary agency (headed by his wife) have exercised over his published and unpublished writings, he was happy to let the Naval Institute Press bring out a limited edition of *The Caine Mutiny* in 1984.

2. Cf. Arnold Beichman, *Herman Wouk: The Novelist as Social Historian* (New Brunswick, N.J.: Transaction Books, 1984), 6; hereafter cited in the text.

3. *The Caine Mutiny* (Garden City, NY: Doubleday, 1951), unnumbered page following title page. For quotations from *The Caine Mutiny* I have used the hardbound edition available from Doubleday. This text is the same as that of the first edition and subsequent printings, though the page numbers vary from printing to printing, and between hardback and paperback.

4. Cf. Beichman, 43. Beichman summarizes a memorandum that Lieutenant Wouk wrote to the Secretary of the Navy in July 1945, outlining problems reservist officers encountered on active duty. Wouk suggested that junior officers be allowed to provide periodic reports on the performance of their commanders—and that such documents not be shared with the commander. Such egalitarian sentiments probably did not receive serious consideration by a military hierarchy which continues to rely on the authority of command position to exact obedience and direct the actions of subordinates in times of crisis.

5. F. I. Carpenter, "Herman Wouk," *College English* 17 (1956), 213; hereafter cited in the text.

6. Albert Van Nostrand, *The Denatured Novel* (New York: Bobbs-Merrill, 1956), 198; hereafter cited in the text. In fairness, it should be noted that for Van Nostrand, "Wouk's novel also disqualifies the ethical problem he poses" (198). Van Nostrand objects to the ending of the novel, in which Barney Greenwald vindicates Queeg and condemns the mutineers.

7. Harvey Swados, "Popular Taste and *The Caine Mutiny*," *Partisan Review* 20 (1953), 252; hereafter cited in the text.

8. J. D. Scott, review of *The Caine Mutiny, New Statesman*, 17 November 1951, 568; hereafter cited in the text.

9. Lydia McClean, "The Incredible Voyage of the 'Caine,' " *Vogue*, 1 February 1953, 194; hereafter cited in the text.

10. Robert Bierstedt, "The Tergiversation of Herman Wouk," *Great*

Moral Dilemmas in Literature, Past and Present, ed. R. M. MacIver (New York: Harper & Bros., 1956), 1; hereafter cited in the text.

11.   Though I have not been able to collect examples of syllabi that include the novel, the presence of F. I. Carpenter's 1956 article on Wouk in both *College English* and the *English Journal* (a publication for high school teachers) suggests that there was strong pedagogical interest in *The Caine Mutiny* in the years immediately following its publication. In the same year that Carpenter published articles in both national journals devoted to teaching literature, *College English* also published James R. Browne, "Distortion in *The Caine Mutiny*" (*College English* 17 [1956], 216–18; hereafter cited in the text). Twenty years later, the *English Journal* published another brief article on the novel by Beverly Haley (*English Journal* 65 [January 1976], 71–72; hereafter cited in the text). Also, if I may be permitted a personal anecdote, I was first introduced to the novel in 1963 in my high school American literature class, where it joined *The Scarlet Letter, The House of the Seven Gables, Billy Budd, A Farewell to Arms*, and *The Red Pony* as required reading.

12.   Having taught the novel in the Naval Academy's "Literature of the Sea" course, I can personally attest to *The Caine Mutiny*'s continuing appeal to young men and women interested in command at sea. Most students, though, are more interested in the value of the book as a lesson in leadership than in its literary merits. Nonetheless, because they are interested in the subject, many midshipmen are easily led to see how literature "works" to illustrate human conflict and illuminate human values. Civilian instructors—two-thirds of the English Department faculty—seem a bit more reluctant to teach the novel, since its literary value is, in their minds, somewhat questionable.

There is also a certain irony in the appearance of the novel, play, and movie in the navy's training courses and at the Naval Academy, since the navy "publicly objected" to the filming of the novel "because it makes the obvious point that a mentally disturbed man not only could remain a naval officer but also could be put in command of a ship" (William H. Brown, Jr., "*The Caine Mutiny*," *Magill's Survey of Cinema* [Englewood Cliffs, N.J.: Salem Press, 1980], 275).

13.   Spencer Brown, "A Code of Honor for a Mutinous Era," *Commentary* (June 1952), 596; hereafter cited in the text.

14.   William H. Whyte, *The Organization Man* (New York: Doubleday, 1956), 246.

15.   Carpenter also believes that Wouk's portrait of Queeg "owes something to Dickens" (Carpenter, 212).

16.   Peter G. Jones, *War and the Novelist: Appraising the American War Novel* (Columbia: University of Missouri Press, 1976), 79; hereafter cited in the text.

17.   W. J. Stuckey, *The Pulitzer Prize Novels: A Critical Backward Look* (Norman, Okla.: University of Oklahoma Press, 1966), 158; hereafter cited in the text.

18.   "*The Caine Mutiny*," *Catholic World* 173 (September 1951), 473.

19. For additional information on this theme, see J. D. Scott's *New Statesman* review (cited above), and "Outcast Ship and Crew," *Atlantic Bookshelf* 188 (August 1951), 79.

20. Rhoda Metraux, "*The Caine Mutiny*," *Explorations* 5 (1956), 36; hereafter cited in the text.

21. At a meeting with his mother in San Francisco long after his father's death, Willie learns that she had known of his father's aspirations, and of Dr. Keith's romance with another woman. She assures Willie that Dr. Keith's longing for a life as a researcher was simply idle dreaming, that he loved the life of luxury (*CM*, 223). Throughout the novel, Willie must fight to overcome the dominance of his mother—no small task, given his profound psychological dependence on her. In fact, as he waits apprehensively for his court-martial to start, he thinks that all will turn out fine because his mother will get him out of this scrape as she has so often done before (*CM*, 391).

22. There is, of course, much of the real-life Herman Wouk in the novelist's portrait of Willie Keith. Though Wouk had tried before Pearl Harbor to join the navy, his real motivation for signing up in early 1942, he indicated to a newspaper reporter 30 years later, was "highly patriotic—I got a note from my draft board." Like Willie, he suffered physical ailments that might have been disqualifying, but with the help of sympathetic doctors—including his own brother, who gave him medication for his high pulse rate—he managed to "bull" his way into service (Frank Young, "Wouk Tells Middies: 'When in doubt, bull,' " *Evening Capital* [Annapolis, Md.], 15 March 1972, 1).

23. For commentary on Wouk's use of the *Alice in Wonderland* motif, see Jones, 67–79.

24. To those who have never served in the military, the probability of a commander's being seen as a kindly father seems low, due to many stories about the brutality of commanders that often circulate in nonmilitary circles. Nevertheless, the American military has perpetuated this notion for at least a century. The *Marine Officer's Guide* quotes this advice for new officers, penned by an early commandant of the Marine Corps: "The relation between officers and enlisted men should in no sense be that of superior and inferior nor that of master and servant, but rather . . . it should partake of the nature of the relation between father and son, to the extent that officers, especially commanding officers, are responsible for the physical, mental, and moral welfare, as well as the discipline and training of the young men under their command" (quoted in R. D. Heinl, Jr., *Marine Officer's Guide*, 4th ed. [Annapolis, Md.: U.S. Naval Institute Press, 1977], 4).

25. "Herman Wouk," *DLB Yearbook, 1982* (New York: Garland Press, 1982), 385; hereafter cited in the text.

26. "Navy Regs to the Rescue," *Saturday Review*, 31 March 1951, 7.

27. Edgar L. Acken, "The War and Willie Keith," *New York Tribune Book Review*, 18 March 1951, 6.

28. Joseph Waldmeir, *American Novels of the Second World War* (The Hague: Mouton, 1971), 136.

116   NOTES AND REFERENCES

29. *Atlantic Bookshelf*, 79.

30. Jeffrey Walsh, *American War Literature, 1914–Vietnam* (London: Macmillan, 1982), 136; hereafter cited in the text.

31. Willie tells his friend Keggs that no commander could make him do "monkey tricks" (*CM*, 115), and when Keggs defends his commander as a decent skipper who just needs to be understood, Willie replies sarcastically that even Hitler can be excused if you simply "understand" him (*CM*, 117). The scene is included to show Willie's immature bravado—he will do his share of "monkey tricks" under Queeg—but also to offer an explanation of how one manages to endure as a subordinate under a harsh commander.

32. "The Conservative as Novelist: Herman Wouk," *Arizona Quarterly* 15 (1959), 130.

33. Wouk manages to take a stab at psychiatrists—one of his favorite targets—during the court-martial episode, by having Barney Greenwald twist the words of one of the doctors who testify regarding Queeg's behavior. The physician claims that men of ordinary intelligence can do a good job in command; Greenwald prods him into suggesting that it takes greater skills to be a psychiatrist than a naval commander—something that does not sit well with the court-martial board, which consists entirely of naval officers (*CM*, 450–51).

34. W. K. Harrison, "Herman Wouk," *Library Journal* 76 (March 1951), 514.

35. *Catholic World*, 473.

36. Ibid.

37. "Herman Wouk," *Booklist*, 15 April 1951, 294.

38. Bernard Nightingale, *New Statesman*, 8 March 1985, 31.

39. In fairness to Wouk, I should point out that in his own public statements he is not as critical of these writers as others have made him out to be. For Wouk's views, which include his fulsome praise for the novelists of the nineteenth century, see his article "You, Me, and the Novel," *Saturday Review* 29 June 1974, 8–13.

40. Cf. Brooks Atkinson, review of *The Caine Mutiny Court-Martial*, *New York Times*, 21 January 1954, 27.

41. Brooks Atkinson, review of *The Caine Mutiny Court-Martial*, *New York Times*, 31 January 1954, sec. 2, 1.

42. Cf. " 'Caine Mutiny' Preview," *New York Times*, 14 October 1953, 35, for comments about the play's opening in San Diego, and "Wouk Play Bows in East," *New York Times*, 15 December 1953, 52, for remarks on the play's debut in White Plains, New York.

43. " 'Mutiny' in London," *New York Times*, 14 January 1956, 40.

44. Atkinson, January 21, 27.

45. The play enjoyed a major revival in 1983, with noted actor Charlton Heston appearing in the role of Captain Queeg. Reviews both at home and abroad were generally favorable. For a sampling of reviews, see Leo Sauvage, review in *New Leader* 66 (13 June 1983), 20; Catherine Hughes, review in

America 148 (11 June 1983), 460; Brendan Gill, review in *New Yorker* 59 (16 May 1983), 102; and *Variety* 311 (11 May 1983), 106. Another view of the revival is provided by Charlton Heston in his *Beijing Diary* (New York: Simon & Schuster, 1990).

46. Cf. Paul Nathan, "Books into Films," *Publisher's Weekly* 153 (14 February 1948), 996, for a discussion of Wouk's development of the screen treatment of *Slattery's Hurricane*.

47. Bosley Crowther, review of *The Caine Mutiny* movie, *New York Times*, 25 June 1954, 17; hereafter cited in the text.

48. R. A. E. Pickard, *Dictionary of 1,000 Best Films* (New York: Association Press, 1971), 71.

49. The film also features at least one future star in a cameo role—Lee Marvin as the sailor Meatball; similarly, in the original stage production, the role of one of the members of the court-martial board is played by "James Bumgarner"—who went on to fame in television as James Garner.

50. Brown, 276; see also Metraux, 41.

51. Interviews conducted by the author at the U.S. Naval Academy and with military colleagues in Washington, D.C.

Chapter Four

1. William S. Hudson, "Herman Wouk: A Biographical and Critical Study" (Ph.D. diss., George Peabody College, 1969), 247; hereafter cited in text. Hudson provides extensive details of the creation and critical reception of *Marjorie Morningstar*, including lengthy excerpts from Wouk's working notes and from the novelist's unpublished articles. Because I have not been given permission to use the Wouk papers, I have refrained from quoting these sources directly, even though they appear in Hudson's study. I have relied extensively on Hudson's work to provide a summary of the genesis of the novel and to locate information about its critical reception.

2. Hudson provides a detailed summary of the play (Hudson, 248–53).

3. A summary of Dawson's thesis is provided by Hudson, 241–43.

4. Cf. Hudson, 248. Hudson also reports that at least one reader had suggested to Wouk that he write a parallel to *The City Boy*, told from a girl's perspective.

5. John K. Hutchens, "Happy Success Story of Herman Wouk," *New York Herald Tribune Book Review* 34 (4 September 1955), 2.

6. Details of the publication history are provided by Hudson, 244–47.

7. "*Marjorie Morningstar*," *Times Literary Supplement*, 7 October 1955, 594; hereafter cited in the text as *TLS*.

8. Meyer Levin, "Central Park Revisited," *Saturday Review*, 3 September 1955, 10; hereafter cited in the text.

9. R. T. Horchler, "Life and the Dream," *Commonweal*, 4 November 1955, 123; hereafter cited in the text.

10. Allen Guttmann, *The Jewish Writer in America: Assimilation and the Crisis of Identity* (New York: Oxford University Press, 1971), 123; hereafter cited in the text.

11. Robert Fitch, "The Bourgeois and the Bohemian," *Antioch Review* 16 (1956), 317; hereafter cited in the text.

12. Marc Lee Raphael, "From Marjorie to Tevya: The Image of the Jews in American Popular Literature, Theater, and Comedy, 1955–1965," *American Jewish History* 74 (1984), 66; hereafter cited in the text.

13. Mark J. Charney, "Herman Wouk," *DLB Yearbook* (New York: Garland Press, 1982), 385; hereafter cited in the text.

14. Maxwell Geismar, review of *Marjorie Morningstar, New York Times*, 4 September 1955, 1; hereafter cited in the text.

15. "Central Park West: Marjorie Morningstar," *The Reporter*, 22 September 1955, 47.

16. Norman Podhoretz, "The Jew as Bourgeois," *Commentary* (February 1986), 188; hereafter cited in the text.

17. Phyllis Deutsch, "Theater of Mating: Jewish Summer Camps and Cultural Transformation," *American Jewish History* 75 (1986), 308. Deutsch believes the entire summer camp episode is naively handled, and that Wouk "describes rather than analyzes" the situation, overemphasizing the evil nature of the place.

18. Wouk himself thought the novel a greater achievement than *The Caine Mutiny* (cf. Hudson, 244). Meyer Levin considered the novel Wouk's "most solid achievement to date" (Levin, 9). British critic John Metcalf, who in his review of *Marjorie Morningstar* calls Wouk "the most important writer working in America," considers this novel "of considerably greater scope and skill than *The Caine Mutiny*. It is, indeed, damned nearly the Great American Novel (Urban Division); certainly it's closer to that illusory target than anything since Dreiser" (*Spectator*, 7 October 1955, 470, 472; hereafter cited in the text).

19. It would be false to suggest that critics have been pleased with the novel's structure. Albert Van Nostrand cites *Marjorie Morningstar* as "a fair sample of the extremity" to which modern novelists have stylized the technique of substituting "description" for "dramatic illusion"—to the point where reading has become considerably boring (cf. Albert Van Nostrand, *The Denatured Novel* [New York: Bobbs-Merrill, 1956], 208).

20. Marjorie has also been compared to Charlotte Temple, the heroine of a late eighteenth-century American novel by Susanna Rowson. Some critics see her as being much more closely allied to literary forebears in the British tradition, namely the heroines of Samuel Richardson's *Clarissa* and *Pamela* (cf. Fiedler, 256, and Riley Hughes, "*Marjorie Morningstar*," *Catholic World*, 182 [November 1955], 1). Raphael believes that Marjorie turns out to be "nearly as virtuous as . . . Pamela, and her virtue, like Pamela's, was well-rewarded" (Raphael, 67). One important difference that Raphael overlooks, however, is that after Pamela is able to get Squire B—— to promise to reform, she has the

courage to marry him; Marjorie spurns her "squire," Noel, even though he promises to abandon his wanderlust and settle down to a life in the suburbs. Perhaps Marjorie understands too well that men like Noel don't stay reformed for long. Certainly his frequent lapses through the middle sections of the novel have offered more than adequate proof for such a conclusion.

21. Cf. Joseph Cohen, "Wouk's Morningstar and Hemingway's Sun," *South Atlantic Quarterly* 58:2 (Spring 1959), 214; hereafter cited in the text. Cohen believes Airman is a combination of "Robert Cohn and Jake Barnes, but he shares affinities with Frederick Henry, Francis Macomber, and Henry Morgan."

22. Hudson does the most extensive analysis of the implications of Noel's change of name (cf. Hudson, 268–70).

23. F. H. Bullock, *New York Herald Tribune*, 4 September 1955, 1.

24. R. Tuerk, quoted in Robert J. DiPietro and Edward Ifkovic, eds., *Ethnic Perspectives in American Literature* (New York: Modern Language Association, 1983), 153.

25. Earl F. Walbridge, review of *Marjorie Morningstar*, *Library Journal* 80:14 (August 1955), 1699; Nora Magid, "The Girl Who Went Back Home," *New Republic*, 5 September 1955, 20, hereafter cited in text; B. R. McElderry Jr., "The Conservative as Novelist: Herman Wouk," *Arizona Quarterly* 15 (1959), 128; hereafter cited in the text.

26. "Marjorie Morningstar," *New Yorker*, 10 September 1955, 155.

27. Criticism was so harsh that Wouk found it necessary to devote space in *This Is My God* to a defense of the book: "In *Marjorie Morningstar* I did my best to portray a bar mitzvah with accuracy and with affection. I thought I succeeded pretty well"—for which, he acknowledges, he received "most bitter and violent objections" from fellow Jews who thought he had trivialized a sacred ceremony. "There were comic touches in the picture, of course," but he says "these lay in the folkway as it exists, not in the imagination of the writer" (New York: Simon & Schuster, 1959, 113–14; hereafter cited in the text as *TIMG*. A revised edition was issued in paperback in 1986.) Whether such a backhanded compliment to tradition did much to ameliorate the hostility has not yet been documented.

28. Charles Angoff and Meyer Levin, eds., *The Rise of American Jewish Literature* (New York: Simon & Schuster, 1970), 511; hereafter cited in the text. The editors include two chapters from the novel in their anthology: "The Seder" and "The Man She Married."

29. "*Nature's Way*," *Theater Arts*, 41 (December 1957), 25–26.

30. Tom Driver, "Broadway Off and On," *The Christian Century* 74 (20 November 1957), 75.

31. Cf. "*Nature's Way*," *Time* 70 (28 October 1957), 92; "Nature's Way," *Nation* 185 (2 November 1957) 310.

32. "Thinblood Wouk," *Time*, 18 May 1962, 96–97. This brief review points out the many parallels between Wouk's hero and Wolfe.

33. Stanley Kaufmann, "Look Backward, Angel," *New Republic*, 11 June 1962, 24–25; hereafter cited in the text. David Dempsey noted that "the shade of Mark Twain is present too" in Wouk's characterization of his protagonist ("It Didn't Pay to Strike It Rich," *New York Times Book Review*, 13 May 1962, 1; hereafter cited in the text).

34. David Boroff, "Hillbilly Literary Tycoon," *Saturday Review* 45 (19 May 1962), 36; hereafter cited in the text.

35. Cf. Richard P. Krafsur, ed., *"Youngblood Hawke," The American Film Institute Catalog of Motion Pictures* (New York: R. R. Bowker, 1976), 1261.

36. Samuel L. Simon, "Herman Wouk," *Library Journal*, 15 May 1962, 1919 (hereafter cited in the text); *"Youngblood Hawke," Kirkus Reviews* 30 (1962), 333; Frederick H. Guidry, "Wouk's Doorstopper," *Christian Science Monitor*, 24 May 1962, 7 (hereafter cited in the text); William James Smith, "Slugging Along," *Commonweal*, 29 June 1962, 355; *"Youngblood Hawke," New York Herald Tribune Weekly Book Review*, 20 May 1962, 4 (hereafter cited in the text); Boroff, 36; Dempsey, 1.

37. Boroff, 36; Frederick I. Carpenter, "Herman Wouk," *College English*, 17 (1956); Stanley Edgar Hyman, *Standards: A Chronicle of Books for Our Time* (New York: Horizon Press, 1966), 69 (hereafter cited in the text); Kaufmann, 24.

38. "The Gull Reef Club," *Atlantic Monthly*, April 1965, 152.

39. Ibid.

40. *Atlantic Monthly*, July 1962, 109.

41. Simon Raven, *Spectator* 209 (19 October 1962), 601; hereafter cited in the text.

42. Quoted in Charney, 386.

43. Beichman, 28, 57.

44. Robert Gordis, "Religion in One Dimension: The Judaism of Herman Wouk," *Midstream* 6 (Winter 1960), 82; hereafter cited in text.

45. "Faith of Herman Wouk," *Newsweek* 54 (21 September 1959), 121; "The Life of Mr. Abramson," *Time* 74 (21 September 1959), 63; Samuel L. Simon, "Herman Wouk," *Library Journal* 84 (1 September 1959), 2505.

46. Will Herberg, "Confession of Faith," *New York Times Book Review*, 27 September 1959, 50.

47. Peter Buitenhaus, *"Don't Stop the Carnival," New York Times Book Review*, 14 March 1965, 47; hereafter cited in the text.

48. "Paper Man," *Times Literary Supplement* 30 (8 July 1965), 573.

49. *"Don't Stop the Carnival," America*, 8 May 1965, 676; Malcolm Bradbury, "Herman Wouk," *The Penguin Companion to American Literature* (New York: Penguin, 1971), 275; "You Must Go Home Again," *Time*, 5 March 1965, 105.

50. Samuel Simon, review, *Library Journal* 90 (1 April 1965), 1749.

51. Haskel Frankel, "Land of Labels," *Saturday Review* 48 (13 March 1965), 128 (hereafter cited in the text); William B. Hill, "Herman Wouk: *Don't Stop the Carnival*," *Bestsellers* 24 (15 March 1965), 479.

52. "Wouk's Island," *Christian Science Monitor* 57 (29 April 1965), 11.
53. *New Statesman*, 2 July 1965.

Chapter Five

1. Cf. Arnold Beichman, *Herman Wouk: The Novelist as Social Historian* (New Brunswick, N.J.: Transaction Books, 1984), 64; hereafter cited in the text.

2. *Publisher's Weekly* reported that in conjunction with the release of ABC's mini-series on *The Winds of War* in 1982, Pocket Books printed an additional 2,000,000 copies of the novel, to take advantage of renewed interest in the work; at that time there were 5,000,000 copies of *Winds of War* in circulation, and 2,000,000 of *War and Remembrance* ("Pocket Battens Down Its Hatches as 'The Winds of War' Rise Again," *Publishers Weekly*, 26 November 1982; hereafter cited as *Publisher's Weekly*).

3. Cf. Jane Howard, "Herman Wouk Surfaces Again," *Life* LXXI (26 November 1971), 53; hereafter cited in the text.

4. Cf. Jean W. Ross, "Interview with Herman Wouk," *Contemporary Authors*, New Revised Series, VI (Detroit: Gale, 1982), 565–66.

5. Michael Mandelbaum, *Political Science Quarterly* 94 (Fall 1979), 515; hereafter cited in the text.

6. Cf. "Foreword" to *War and Remembrance*; Wouk refers to *The Winds of War* as a romance in his "Foreword" to that novel as well. Several different editions of both novels, both hardcover and paperback, are available. For this study I have used the following: *The Winds of War* (New York: Pocket Books, 1971), cited in the text as *WW*; and *War and Remembrance* (Boston: Little, Brown, 1978), cited in the text as *WR*.

7. A significant body of literature has been written about the historical novel—a bit less about historical romance. The latter has been quite popular in America for the past four decades, with dozens of writers spurred on by the phenomenal success of Margaret Mitchell's *Gone with the Wind*, and its subsequent release as a movie in the 1930s. The century's premier Thackeray scholar, Gordon N. Ray, remarked at mid-century that "historical fiction has fallen into disrepute" because "the genre has been preempted by popular entertainers, who have made its exploitation a major literary industry" (*Thackeray: The Age of Wisdom* [New York: McGraw-Hill, 1958]). The last three decades have seen even more exploitation, as booksellers' shelves have been filled by thick paperbacks set in the antebellum South, the midwestern plains, or exotic locales in Europe, Africa, and Asia. A number of reviewers have simply lumped Wouk's war novels with this class of romance. Readers interested in the development of the historical novel will find a lucid, extensive study of the genre in Avrom Fleishmann, *The English Historical Novel: From Walter Scott to Virginia Woolf* (Baltimore: Johns Hopkins, 1971). A more recent study of the historical writer's craft, informed by contemporary theory, is Barbara Foley's *Telling the Truth: The*

Theory and Practice of Documentary Fiction (Ithaca: Cornell Univ. Press, 1986). A
brief analysis is provided in Laurence W. Mazzeno, "The Historical Novel,"
Critical Survey of Long Fiction, English Language Authors edn. (Englewood Cliffs,
N.J.: Salem Press, 1983), 3150–56.

8. Karen McPherson, "The American Military in Fiction since 1945,"
Armed Forces and Society 9 (Summer 1983), 649; hereafter cited in the text.

9. Richard Bolton, *"The Winds of War* and Wouk's Wish for the
World," *Midwest Quarterly* 16 (1975), 393, 399; hereafter cited in the text.

10. Pearl Bell, "Good-Bad and Bad-Bad," *Commentary* 66 (December
1978), 71; hereafter cited in the text. Bell does not think Wouk is fully successful in realizing this aim, however, since "there is hardly a genuinely ordinary
person" in the Henry family (Bell, 71).

11. Michael Mandelbaum suggests that Wouk's desire to make his hero
a symbol of the Allies is the reason Pug seems at times a bit unbelievable: "If he
is flawed as a fictional creation it is because he is too tough, too down to earth,
too much what his wife Rhoda calls him, '. . . a patriot.' He is too much what he
is because he is a symbol—of the basic decency and strength, of Americans and
America, that stopped Hitler and saved the world from barbarism"
(Mandelbaum, 521).

12. Throughout both novels Wouk draws subtle parallels between
Jastrow's fictional book about Christ and his own study of the Jewish people,
This Is My God. Both are written to explain something about the Jewish faith to
nonbelievers, both are Book-of-the-Month Club selections, and both provide
substantial income to their authors. This is another instance of Wouk's using his
fictional materials to express the significance of his Jewish heritage.

13. While these multiple plots allow Wouk the expansiveness necessary
to capture the scope of the war, they place demands on the reader's attention
span. At times, more than 100 pages interrupt one story with another. Despite
their size, the novels are hard to put down for a long time if readers wish to
keep all the stories straight in their minds.

14. Zhang Yidong provides a detailed comparison of Tolstoy and Wouk
in their methods of plotting and treatment of historical figures in "Two
Panoramas about Great Wars," *Journal of Popular Culture* 19 (Summer 1985),
57–63.

15. About the same battle, Wouk has Alistair Tudsbury refer to
Midway as "the Trafalgar of the Pacific" (*WR*, 262).

16. Barbara Bannon, review of *The Winds of War*, *Publisher's Weekly* 7
February 1972, 44; hereafter cited in text.

17. Wouk tends to stereotype Nazis in much the same way he accuses
them (and the Allies) of stereotyping Jews. He depicts them as boorish, sexual-
ly promiscuous, grotesque, and given to crude jokes and humor; the incident at
the Stoller villa, Abenruh, where all the ladies must enter the dining room by
sliding down the banister as the men watch, is certainly one that feeds the

image of the Nazis as simply complexes of animal appetites (*WW*, 356). Under the circumstances, it is perhaps understandable that the author is unable to see much good in the party and army that exterminated over six million of his kinsmen.

18.   This phrase occurs in Aaron's lecture on Homer's *Iliad*, delivered in the ghetto at Theresienstadt. Aaron is speaking of the heroes of the *Iliad* as pawns in the hands of gods who seem unconcerned about their suffering; their only aim is to amuse themselves by manipulating the figures on the battlefield. One is reminded of Gloucester's lament to King Lear: "As flies to wanton boys, are we to the gods;/They kill us for their sport" (*King Lear*, act 4, sc. 1, lines 36–37).

19.   Aaron's cousin Berel Jastrow is an explicit symbol of the Jewish nation; he survives personal suffering and loss to rise up strong in his fight against the forces of evil. Berel loses his wife, is separated from his family, spends time in a death camp building the gas ovens in which his kinsmen will be exterminated, yet eventually escapes to join the resistance that frees thousands of Jews (including Byron and Natalie's son Louis). Wouk uses Berel to dramatize the quality of endurance that characterizes the entire Jewish race.

20.   "Herman Wouk," *Choice*, June 1972, 512.

21.   "War and Remembrance," *Publisher's Weekly*, 4 September 1978, 102.

22.   Geoffrey Norman, "Wouk on War," *Esquire Magazine* 90 (15 December 1978), 96; hereafter cited in the text.

23.   Paul Fussell, "War and Remembrance," *New Republic*, 14 October 1978, 32; hereafter cited in the text as "Fussell."

24.   P. S. Coyne, "Books in Brief," *National Review*, 14 April 1972, 29.

25.   Melvin Maddocks, "Wouk at War in Slow Motion," *Life*, 26 November 1971, 16; hereafter cited in the text.

26.   Cf. Paul Fussell, *The Great War and Modern Memory* (New York: Oxford, 1976) and *Wartime: Understanding and Behavior in the Second World War* (New York: Oxford, 1989).

27.   Harry F. Waters, "ABC's High-Flying 'Winds,' " *Newsweek*, 7 February 1983, 72.

28.   Cf. "*The Winds of War*—Part One," *Variety*, 9 February 1983, 66; also Gerald Clark, "The $40 Million Gamble," *Time*, 7 February 1983, 70.

29.   An excellent discussion of the production, including information on casting and the problems encountered during the 13 months of shooting, is in "Pocket Battens down Its Hatches," *Publisher's Weekly*, cited above.

30.   "Wages of War," *Time*, 28 February 1983, 63; hereafter cited as *Time*.

31.   James Wolcott, "Windy," *New York*, 7 February 1983, 76.

32.   Quoted in "$40 Million Gamble," 74.

Chapter Six

1. An earlier version of my discussion of *Inside, Outside* appeared in a review of the novel in *Magill's Literary Annual, 1986* (Englewood Cliffs, N.J.: Salem Press, 1987), 466–69. For other opinions of the novel, see R. Z. Shepherd, *Time* 125 (1 April 1985), 79; and James A. Michener, *New York Times Book Review* 90 (10 March 1985), 1.

2. Herman Wouk, *Inside, Outside* (Boston: Little Brown, 1985), 158; hereafter cited in the text as *Inside*.

3. Arnold Kettle, *An Introduction to the English Novel*, vol. 2 (London: Hutchinson University Library, 1967), 60.

4. Wouk's remarks are quoted in Cleveland Amory, "Trade Winds," *Saturday Review* 55 (12 February 1972), 8.

5. Cf. Barbara Bannon, review of *The Winds of War*, *Publisher's Weekly* 201 (7 February 1972), 44–50.

6. As I mentioned in my preface, Wouk has placed a considerable amount of manuscript material in the archives at Columbia University. He has not made these documents public, and the library is not able to allow inspection of any of this material without specific permission from the author.

Selected Bibliography

PRIMARY SOURCES

Published Works

Fiction

Aurora Dawn; or, The True History of Andrew Reale, Containing a Faithful Account of the Great Riot, Together with the Complete Texts of Michael Wilde's Oration and Father Stanfield's Sermon. New York: Simon & Schuster, 1947.
The Caine Mutiny. New York: Doubleday, 1951.
The City Boy. New York: Doubleday, 1948.
Don't Stop the Carnival. New York: Doubleday, 1965.
Inside, Outside. Boston: Little, Brown, 1985
The "Lokomoke" Papers. Collier's, 1956. [New York: Pocket Books, 1968.]
Marjorie Morningstar. New York: Doubleday, 1955.
War and Remembrance. Boston: Little, Brown, 1978.
The Winds of War. Boston: Little, Brown, 1971.
Youngblood Hawke. New York: Doubleday, 1962.

Dramatic Works

The Caine Mutiny Court-Martial. New York: Doubleday, 1954.
Natures' Way. Garden City, N.Y.: Doubleday, 1958.
Slattery's Hurricane. Screen treatment, 1948. New York: Pocket Books, 1956.
The Traitor. New York: Samuel French, 1949.

Nonfiction

Book

This Is My God. Garden City, N.Y.: Doubleday, 1959; paperback edition 1986.

Articles and Parts of Books

"Introduction." *Self-Portrait of a Hero: The Letters of Jonathan Netanyahu.* New York: Random House, 1980.
"On Being Put under Glass," *Columbia University Columns* 5 (1956):3–9.
"You, Me, and the Novel." *Saturday Review,* 29 June 1974, 8–13.

Cinematic and Television Adaptations

The Caine Mutiny (movie).

The Winds of War (television mini-series).
War and Remembrance (television mini-series).

Unpublished Works

A considerable amount of material, now filling 61 boxes, is housed in the Butler Library, Columbia University, New York. Included are journals, letters to and from correspondents, working notes, drafts, and unpublished letters and plays. Access to this material is restricted.

SECONDARY SOURCES

Book

Beichman, Arnold. *Herman Wouk: The Novelist as Social Historian.* New Brunswick, N.J.: Transaction Books, 1984. Brief monograph by Wouk's close friend; chiefly concerned with defending Wouk's conservative political and philosophical outlook. Includes some important observations based on material in the Wouk collection at Columbia University.

Articles, Parts of Books, and Reviews

Bierstedt, Robert. "The Tergiversation of Herman Wouk." in *Great Moral Dilemmas*, edited by R. M. MacIver, 1–14. New York: Harper & Bros., 1956. Focuses on the moral issues of *The Caine Mutiny*, emphasizing the implications of Maryk's decision to relieve Queeg.
Bolton, Richard R. "*The Winds of War* and Wouk's Wish for the World." *Midwest Quarterly* 16 (1975): 389–408. A balanced critical analysis of the novel, showing how Wouk uses structure, characterization, and incident to achieve a moral purpose. Detailed discussion of Wouk's success in creating Victory Henry as the ideal professional naval officer.
Brown, Spencer R. "A Code of Honor for a Mutinous Era." *Commentary* (June 1952): 595–99. Examination of *The Caine Mutiny* focusing on Wouk's treatment of the problem of power and responsibility.
Carpenter, Frederick I. "Herman Wouk." *College English* 17:iv (January 1956): 211–15. [Reprinted as "Herman Wouk and the Wisdom of Disillusion." *English Journal* 45 (1956): 1–6, 32.] Brief assessment of Wouk's early work, focusing on *The Caine Mutiny*; attempts to place Wouk within the modern tradition, but faults him for being too moralistic.
Cohen, Joseph. "Wouk's Morningstar and Hemingway's Sun," *South Atlantic Quarterly* 58, no. 2 (Spring 1959): 213–24. Develops parallels between *Marjorie Morningstar* and Hemingway's writings, especially *The Sun Also Rises*; sees Noel Airman as a kind of Hemingway hero.

Darby, William. *Necessary American Fictions: Popular Literature of the 1950s*, 43–55. Bowling Green, Oh.: Bowling Green State University Popular Press, 1987. Examines *The Caine Mutiny* as an example of the way best-selling novels of the 1950s mirror American values of the period; provides careful assessment of Wouk's characterization in the novel.

Fitch, Robert E. "The Bourgeois and the Bohemian." *Antioch Review* 16, no. 2 (June 1956): 131–45. Critical analysis of *Marjorie Morningstar*; sees the novel as portraying the conflict between two prevailing ideologies, each dominating in a section of society: the moralistic middle class (bourgeois) and the liberal intellectual community (bohemian).

Gordis, Robert. "Religion in One Dimension: The Judaism of Herman Wouk." *Midstream* 6, no. 1 (Winter 1960), 82–90. Detailed review of *This Is My God*; highlights the faults of Wouk's study of Judaism, while acknowledging its merits.

Hyman, Stanley Edgar. *Standards: A Chronicle of Books for Our Time*, 68–72. New York: Horizon Press, 1966. Savage review of *Youngblood Hawke*, which faults Wouk for contrived plotting, weak characterization, squeamishness in dealing with sexual issues, and pandering to a nonthinking reading public. An important article for those wishing to see the extreme reaction Wouk has evoked in some critical circles.

Jones, Peter G. *War and the Novelist: Appraising the American War Novel*, 73–79. Columbia, Mo.: University of Missouri Press, 1976. Discusses *The Caine Mutiny* as paradigmatic of novels dealing with the problem of military command.

McElderry, B. R. "The Conservative as Novelist: Herman Wouk." *Arizona Quarterly* 15 (1959): 128–36. Focusing on *The Caine Mutiny* and *Marjorie Morningstar*, McElderry discusses the way Wouk integrates conservative values into his novels.

Metraux, Rhoda. "*The Caine Mutiny*." *Explorations* 5 (1956): 36–44. Examines major themes in the novel; makes brief comparison between the novel and the film adaptation.

Milne, Gordon. *Ports of Call: A Study of the American Nautical Novel*, 77–89. Lanham, Md.: University Press of America, 1986. Devotes a chapter to *The Caine Mutiny, The Winds of War*, and *War and Remembrance* as examples of the way one author uses naval operations in World War II to explore human reactions to war.

Stuckey, W. J. *The Pulitzer Prize Novels*, 158–64. Norman, Okla.: University of Oklahoma Press, 1966. Analysis of *The Caine Mutiny* in which Wouk is faulted for attacking intellectuals through his portrait of Keefer.

Swados, Harry. "Popular Taste and *The Caine Mutiny*." *Partisan Review* 20 (1953): 248–56. Analysis of the novel as an appeal to the new middle class that emerged in America after World War II, a reading public that did not wish to think much or to have its values challenged.

Waldmeir, Joseph J. *American Novels of the Second World War*, 124–37. The Hague: Mouton, 1971. Sees Wouk's *The Caine Mutiny* and James Gould Cozzens's *Guard of Honor* as representing minority points of view about the war, in that they celebrate the importance of subordinating individual freedom to authority. Notes the difficulties that the novel presents in the famous reversal scene in which Greenwald defends Queeg after the court-martial.

Whyte, William H. *The Organization Man*, 243–48. New York: Doubleday, 1956. Analysis of *The Caine Mutiny*, critical of Wouk's decision to blame Maryk and absolve Queeg of all responsibility for the mutiny.

"The Wouk Mutiny." *Time*, 5 September 1955, 48–52. Prompted by the publication of *Marjorie Morningstar*, this important cover story provides biographical details and Wouk's own comments on his novels; outlines Wouk's commitment to conservative American values.

Zhang Yidong. "Two Panoramas about Great Wars." *Journal of Popular Culture* 19, no. 1 (Summer 1985): 57–63. A comparison of Wouk's World War II novels (*The Winds of War* and *War and Remembrance*) with Tolstoy's *War and Peace*.

Index

The Author

Laurence W. Mazzeno is vice president for Academic Affairs and academic dean at Ursuline College, Pepper Pike, Ohio. A native of New Orleans, Louisiana, he received his B.A. from Loyola University in 1968 and his Ph.D. from Tulane University in 1978. He served on the faculties at the U.S. Military Academy and the U.S. Naval Academy, where he was chair of the English Department from 1986 to 1989. From 1989 to 1992 he was a dean at Mesa State College in Grand Junction, Colorado. He has published widely on British and American authors and has compiled *The Victorian Novel* (1989) and *Victorian Poetry* (1994) in the Magill's Literary Bibliography Series. For eight years he was an editor for *The Arnoldian: A Review of Mid-Victorian Culture*; from 1988 to 1992 he edited *Nineteenth-Century Prose*, a journal featuring scholarship on nonfiction prose of the nineteenth century.

The Editor

Frank Day is a professor of English at Clemson University. He is the author of *Sir William Empson: An Annotated Bibliography* and *Arthur Koestler: A Guide to Research*. He was a Fulbright lecturer in American literature in Romania (1980–81) and in Bangladesh (1986–87).